# WHAT SHALL I CRY?

## BELINDA HOOD

PRESS

*What Shall I Cry?*
by Belinda Hood

Printed in the United States of America

ISBN 9781613799482

www.xulonpress.com

# CONTENTS

# DEDICATION

## ⋮

This book is wholeheartedly dedicated to
God the Father;
God the Son; God the Holy Spirit!

May your Name be forever glorified!

THANK YOU LORD FOR YOUR FAITHFULNESS
AND LOVE. MAY ALL YOUR CREATION
BLESS YOUR NAME!

# ACKNOWLEDGMENTS

:
•

## THANKS...

A special thanks to my husband Greg; through it all – GOD HAS BEEN FAITHFUL! You have been such a tower of strength, love and patience to and for me. God bless you – God's Man of Love, Faith and Power!

Much, much, much, much love and thanks to my sons: Myron, Michael, Marlon and Markus. Our family has weathered many storms! I thank God that we did not allow the enemy to wreck our family. I thank God that all of you have been restored; that you have continued to walk in love and that you have kept your faith in God -DESPITE the "arrows" that were thrown at all of us! I thank you for understanding the NEED to write this book and allowing yourselves to be put on "front street". You are truly my "Sons of Issachar"; and Sons of the Most High God! God bless you all!

Much heartfelt thanks, gratitude and love for my Love In Action Family; and my "family" of friends. You all stayed with me and my family – THROUGH ALL THE TESTS! You continued to show AGAPE love to our family. You kept the prayer lines open day and night. You stood firm in your faith and did not "come down off the wall!" You kept your Sword by your side and helped fight the "Sanballats and Tobias's" that came our way. You genuinely and sincerely put your LOVE IN ACTION! I shall always be eternally grateful and thankful for your love, support, compassion and prayers. I pray that God will "remember" your labor of love and reward your faithfulness. May God continue to bless and keep you all!

A special thanks to the precious young women in my life that the Lord used to help me walk in unconditional love. You may have thought that I was helping you, BUT GOD used you as the "instruments" to shape and mold my battered frame of mind and broken spirit. I love you all. May God be the Center of your joy!

Very special thanks to the precious little ones that have come into my life! You are welcome into my heart and into our home. Nana loves you so very, very much!

## TO GOD BE THE GLORY!

# PREFACE

⋮
●

"In the same way, the Spirit helps us in our weakness. We do
not know what we ought to pray for, but the Spirit Himself
intercedes for us with groans that words cannot express.
And He who searches our hearts knows the mind of the
Spirit, because the Spirit intercedes for the saints in
accordance with God's will."
Romans 8:26-27

The pages of our history books are filled with criers – those
who warned of impending dangers (Paul Revere and
William Dawes); and those who cried out for justice (Martin L.
King, Jr. and President John F. Kennedy), just to name a few.

The Bible is also filled with criers. The prophets of old were
aptly called by God -"watchmen". They would see danger
approaching and warn the city. They would go into the "kings"
of the earth and cry out against the injustices of God's people.
They would also warn the people of their wickedness towards
God and declare their appropriate fate.

John the Baptist was one such crier. His cry was, "REPENT
FOR THE KINGDOM OF HEAVEN IS AT HAND." He cried
out for a turning away from evil – and a turning towards the only
True and Living God! John the Baptist was also aptly called the
"forerunner" of Jesus Christ. He cried out for holiness – God's
holiness!

Jesus, our Lord and Savior, was a crier. He cried out for Truth – God's Truth. Sadly, His cries fell on many "religious" ears; those whose ears were deaf to the shrill of holiness and Truth.

"The Pharisees came and began to question Jesus. To test him, they asked him for a sign from heaven."
Mark 8:11

"Be careful, Jesus said to them. Be on your guard against the yeast of the Pharisees and Sadducees."
*Matthew 16:6*

Yet the cry of Jesus was heard and received by those that desired salvation; those that believed that Jesus was (and is) truly the Word, the Life, and the Light – that is He IS the Christ, the Son of God!

"Yet to all who received Him, to those who believed in his name, he gave the right to become children of God."
*John 1:12*

Jesus cried over Jerusalem; the city of the King! (*see Luke 13:34-35*) He also cried as His Spirit was deeply moved by the mourning of Mary and Martha (the sisters of Lazarus) and the others who mourned with them. His compassion for their pain moved Him to tears.

"JESUS WEPT."
*John 11:35*

Oh — the tears of our Savior! And yes beloved – there's a lot (today) to cry about!

Throughout the ages there have been criers; those that make proclamations or announcements for his or her town or community. The traditional opening word of the criers were "OYEZ" (oh yeah) which means "to hearken" or "hear ye"; and Church we need such criers today! OH YEAH! OH YEAH!

To CRY means to: make a loud or shrill sound, especially to express pain, grief, etc. or to appeal for help; to shed tears; weep; say or exclaim loudly or excitedly.

There are various reasons to cry. Some of us cry when we are happy; tears of joy! Some of us cry when we are sad; tears of sorrow! Some of us cry when we are excited; involuntary tears! Some of us cry when we are uncertain; I'm thinking too hard tears! And some of us cry when we are extremely burdened- with a burden that only God can see or understand; tears of pain – tears of the heart!

Whatever the reason, or the season — we cry! Some cry more than others. I think of myself as a crybaby; one who frequently sheds tears. I do not cry for foolish or selfish reasons; I'm not THAT emotional! But whenever I sit and speak to the Lord; whenever I consider the present state of the Church of Jesus Christ and this world in general – I CRY! (I know- that's a lot to cry about!) I cry for so many reasons. The primary reason is that we – THE BODY OF CHRIST – are so "estranged" from our husband – Jesus Christ. We have "left our first love" and have gone whoring after the "gods" of this world! It is a sad, but true, commentary. And yes – I cry!

When I think of ALL that our Heavenly Father has done for us: giving us His Only Son (*see John 3:16*); forgiving mankind for all our sins and reconciling us back to Himself (*see II Corinthians 5:19*); Jesus dying on the Cross for all mankind; shedding His innocent blood for sinners like you and I – I can't help but cry! What a price Jesus paid for me, for us!

When I think of the years that I personally wasted on riotous living, foolishness, selfishness and so on (like the prodigal son noted in *Luke 15:11-32*) – I cry tears of thankfulness and gratitude. God did not have to allow me to keep on living. My lifestyle was anti-God. He did not have to keep demonstrating His love towards me. He could have allowed me to die in my sin. BUT GOD! God saw fit to send His Holy Spirit into my dark world and draw me unto Himself! My Heavenly Father was right there waiting for me with His arms wide open. PRAISE GOD!

I cry because so many Christians have not come back home! They are still enjoying the pleasures of sin! They do not know (or believe) that the pleasures of sin are only for a season; a short time. But beloved, let me assure you they are; this too shall pass. Time has a way of making sure that everything that we see is temporal and subject to change. I cry because the change seems to be extremely gradual, so extremely painful and extremely short-termed. WE FORGET GOD! We seem to have forgotten the eternal words of God via the Bible. We have made a "conscious" decision to "alter" God's Word. We have inserted our own vernacular, we have superintended our own thoughts over the Holy Spirit's interpretation of His Word and we have re-written the Holy Bible to suit ourselves! Holy is defined as: morally and spiritually excellent or perfect; to be revered; belonging to, devoted to, or empowered by God.

So many Christians today are out looking for "bargains"; window shopping. They want a "reduced" gospel message and a "two-for-one" place of worship. They have "peeked" in to see IF they can agree with the "price" and yet decided to continue to shop. They are spectators! They ask, "Can you hold this for me?" "I will come back and get it later". Needless to say – they never return. And what about the ones that "buy" the product, keep the tags on, use it – and then return it for a refund? They are the users! They use the Church for their own personal gain. They ask, "What is in it for me?" Isn't that selfish? Don't you feel the tears streaming down your face? Or have you become immune to these atrocities?

You see beloved – today there are many Christians who have become immune to, accustomed to, partakers of and comfortable in SIN! Oh no – we don't dare call it sin – that's not being politically correct! And so – I CRY!

# WHERE DO I BEGIN?

### "The line of attraction is always the line of appeal."

. . .

**GIRL - I TOLD YOU THAT BOY AIN'T READY!**

Ahhh——those words have rang out from the mouths of many mothers. Mothers who have tried to warn, teach, understand and save the heartaches and pains of many young ladies; the many young ladies who love hard and fall prey to sin - namely sexual sin.

Many mothers (fathers, guardians) can attest to making this statement. But many have seen the declension and ruin of precious lives due to the hardening of the heart, the inability to say no and/or the lack of spiritual submission.

So - where do I begin? What is my heart's cry? What do these words mean to me?

Well - I am a mother, a grandmother, a mentor and a friend to many young ladies. I am also a Woman of God, and I have sons. I want to preface this writing by stating some facts. According to the Illinois Census Bureau – approximately _75%_ of American households are maintained or headed by females. These are startling statistics?

Women (females) share the brunt of most of the "after effects" of sexual immorality, namely because they are the ones who become pregnant. HOWEVER, it does not negate the father's (males) responsibilities toward their child/children.

Statistics also report that: depression ranks highest among females: a ratio of 2:1. Again, these are alarming statistics. Yet, these statistics are expected to increase in percentages and ration within 2-3 years; then annually.

Personally, I am a staunch advocate of abstinence (the act of abstaining- refraining from indulging especially from food, alcohol or sexual relations). (In this matter we are addressing sexual relations.) ). THERE IS NO SAFE SEX!

GOD'S WORD SAYS—

"Flee the evil desires of youth, and pursue righteousness, faith, love and peace, along with those who call on the Lord out of a pure heart."
*II Timothy 2:22*

"Flee from sexual immorality. All other sins a man (*woman*) commits are outside his (*her*) body, but he (*she*) who sins sexually sins against his (*her*) own body."
*I Corinthians 6:18 (italics added)*

Joseph is a young man's example of how to "run" from sin. (*see Genesis- Chapter 39*) We all could learn some pivotal lessons from him. Sadly, in today's culture, the great majority of our youths are running towards sin! I also advocate abstinence because God, by His Word, commands holy living.

"But just as He who called you is holy, so be holy in all you do; for it is written: Be holy, because I am holy."
*I Peter 1:15-16*

"For God did not call us to be impure, but to live a holy life. Therefore, he who rejects this instruction does not reject man but God, who gives you his Holy Spirit."
*I Thessalonians 4:7-8*

## QUESTION: HAS GOD CHANGED HIS MIND ABOUT SIN AND SEX?

"I the Lord do not change."(*Malachi 3:6a*) DOES IT SOUND LIKE HE HAS?

Back to the opening statement: GIRL I TOLD YOU THAT BOY AIN'T READY!

There are many mothers that believe their sons are "too good" for some of the young ladies/women of today. They have a tendency to check out or scrutinize the young ladies/women's entire heritage. Please understand: there is nothing wrong or inappropriate when a mother, father or guardian desires the best for their children. Most of us know that our DNA is powerful! There are generations of sickness, disease, murder, mental health, etc. in our blood lines, and parents should be cautious. But there is definitely something wrong or inappropriate when a parent, namely the mother, believes in her heart that no one is "good enough" for her son; that she must be involved in every choice that her son makes; that she alone knows what is best for her son; and that she uses her matriarchal dominance to control him. The truth of the matter is - some mothers do not know that the umbilical cord was cut at birth, and that they must now allow their son(s) to grow up!

## CAN WE TALK?

Let me ask you a question - what specifically comes to mind when you hear the statement, "Oh, he's just a mama's boy!" (Think carefully now.) Well, I believe that sometimes when we call a young man a mama's boy- it can really be a good thing. Here's why:

First of all - it tells me that he loves his mama. That's a good thing.

Secondly - that he respects his mama. That's another good thing.

Thirdly - that he wants to please his mama and that he will listen to her words of wisdom - and obey them! That's definitely a good thing!

And lastly (but not finally) - that he values his mama's presence. I mean - he looks forward to being around the woman that "housed" his unseen body; the woman that nurtured and nourished him; the woman that shielded him from life's everyday nuisances; the woman that could make all his wrongs seem right; the woman that taught him proper etiquette - Sit up straight! Don't talk with your mouth full! Clean that dirty room! I'm sure that you know what I mean. That too is a good thing.

The mama's boy that I envision sees his mother through the eyes of God. He knows that, other than God, no one could love him more. He also knows that mama will always love and forgive him - no matter what! A mother's love goes a long way!

However, I am not naïve. I know that there are many others that view a mama's boy from a very different perspective; in a very different light. Some believe him to be - henpecked, too sheltered, always relying on his mama, can't make a move without his mama's approval, and compares every woman/ young lady to his mama - the list is inexhaustive! It is also true that many young men have hid behind their mama's skirt tails. Whenever their relationships go awry they run to their mamas. Now - that's another term - I dare not use!

But there is a "special" something about a boy and his mama. It starts when she is carrying him in her womb. There is great joy and adoration at the thought of her carrying a man child! It warms the mother's heart to feel her son inside of her. It is inexpressionable!

HOWEVER, there are times in a mother's life when her little boy seems foreign, distant and out of touch. In her heart she wonders, "Is this really my child?" She wonders and cries to herself, "What happened to my child?" The realization is inevitable. LIFE! Life has happened to her boy, (her girl). Yes - by the grace of God, life happens to all children. Life will deal all of us some serious blows. Life will cause us to want to run and hide, to cry rivers of tears, to become angry, to be ashamed, to be embarrassed and to cry out to God for help and consolation. Yes - life is as real as it gets. Welcome mothers - TO THE REAL WORLD!

I believe that the Holy Spirit has penned this writing. I believe that He is directing me to share my experiences and to "free me"; to free me from the pangs of hurt, pride, shame and disgrace. But God also wants to help others; those who believe that they are unable to live holy in an unholy world. In essence, God wants to "grow us up" and enable us to love unconditionally, just as He loves all of us through His Son -Jesus Christ. I believe that He wants this from all of His children.

My husband Greg and I have four sons; I also have a bonus son. So we have a total of five sons; five young men; five personalities; five unique characters and five young men who are very much like their father. GOD HELP ME!

As any mother can attest, children can be born, nurtured, reared and loved by the same parents, in the same home - YET -they can be totally different. (I hear those AMENS.) Each one is unique and special. (Special in a good way - I hear you!)

Well - raising four sons has been a tremendous joy, and a tremendous challenge. Those with boys know what I mean. Boys are ALWAYS testing you!

They test your patience: Stop that!

They test your sanity: What did you say?

They test your energy: Don't move from that spot!

They test your decision making: Did I say you could go there?

And they test your love: I know sweetheart - you didn't mean to kill the cat!

But tests, or challenges, are meant to help us, as parents, to grow. If we will allow the tests, they will take us to the next level; falls and all. The very growth process of our children are life-lessons, and challenges. And yes – growth pains!

In the "terrible two" stage they challenge us with toileting and talking.

In the toddler stage they challenge us with food fights and quick napping.

In the primary stage they challenge us with separation anxiety, entering school, etc.

In the teenage stage - oh what a challenge!

In the young adult stage life challenges them - and guess what? They challenge us!

During each stage of our lives we are challenged. (Hey- is that fair?) The truth is - children will be on your heart until the day that YOU die. There is a bonding that nothing and no one can separate. Only God has a greater bond in our hearts than our children. And it is to God that every parent must go to understand, what we call, the complex makings of our children.

Back to my sons. As of this writing they are grown ups, ranging from ages 23-40. I also have seven grandchildren; but there's more! I sense a digression here - but I promise you - I will come back to the crux.

# CHAPTER ONE

⋮
●

"There is no such thing as a private life – "a world within the world" – for a man or woman who is brought into fellowship with Jesus Christ's sufferings. God breaks up the private life of His saints, and makes it a thoroughfare for the world on the one hand and for Himself on the other. No human being can stand that unless he is identified with Jesus Christ."
(Oswald Chambers)

First, let's look at my background and lay a biblical foundation. To reiterate - I am a Woman of God. I love the Lord! I have been saved (a born-again Christian) for over 30 years. I gave my heart to the Lord after the birth of my second son. I came to know Christ at the age of 25. I grew up in the church; attended church all my life. I sang in the choir and attended Sunday School on a regular basis. In essence, I knew OF Christ. Going to church was a given, a constant and a commandment. It was not an option. So, as a "church girl", I knew the spiritual jargon. I knew the expectation of my mama, the church folks and the world. There are just certain things that church girls don't do! Amen?

In essence, I played church; it was a game to me. When I was a youth I had an imaginary world; I lived a life of fantasies. As stated, I did not have an option with regards to church; I had to go - like it or not. I would constantly fantasize about things that church girls weren't allowed to think or permitted to do. I had my own world. In my world I was in charge; no one could dictate to me where to go or who to be with- it was MY world. And I lived it out!

## PROBLEM: FANTASIES ARE NOT REAL!

Fantasy as defined by The Oxford American Dictionary of Current English: the faculty of inventing images, especially extravagant or visionary ones, a fanciful mental image, a day-dream, a whimsical speculation, pretense, make-believe.

Yes, I lived it and I loved it! Sadly, these fantasies -this make-believe life- was carried over to my adult life. I just could not, and would not, let them go. For me - they were my safety and security. It was extremely hard for me to discern the reality. I was embedded in pretense. But what I failed to realize was that this whimsical world was setting the stage for my future demise. (But that's another book.)

"But he who chases fantasies lack judgment."
*Proverbs 12:11b*

"But the one who chases fantasies will have his fill of poverty."
*Proverbs 28:19b*

Many psychologists and psychiatrists tell us that there is nothing wrong with children having imaginary playmates. Some have gone so far as to "caution" parents that want to interfere in their children's imaginary world. For the record - I am not a psychologist or psychiatrist. I will not condemn, belittle or refute these professionals. I believe that this is a necessary and viable profession. However, what I can attest to, from past experiences and what I have learned about the spiritual world, is that there is a great contrast between angels that are sent by God to minister to us (*see Hebrews 1:14*) and demons that masquerade as angels of light (*see II Corinthians 11:14*). I now know that demons can take on any form. I also know that the mind is the devil's battlefield, and especially for a child - his playground.

A spirit-filled adult may have discernment, but a child does not. Satan is subtle (evasive or mysterious, hard to grasp, ingenious). We must be alert, sober, and watchful at all times.

"Be self-controlled and alert. Your enemy the devil prowls around like a roaring lion looking for someone to devour."
*I Peter 5:8*

"So then, let us not be like others, who are asleep, but let us be alert and self-controlled."
*I Thessalonians 5:6*

These so called "friends" that I encountered in my fantasy world refused to go away. They became part of me; they dictated their plans to me and like a dumb sheep I followed them to the slaughter. I was at their mercy. BUT GOD! It takes the power of the Holy Spirit to set you free. Praise God!

(I KNOW - I DIGRESSED. THAT'S A DIFFERENT BOOK ALSO.)

When I accepted Jesus Christ as my Savior - I began to really see the Jesus that was talked about in church; He came to life. Or rather - I came to life. It was I who was dead in sin and trespasses. The Bible was no longer pages of red and black letters - they became His Word - Spirit and Life! I later learned that Jesus had to be more to me than a Savior - He had to be my Lord; Ruler of my life. I believe that this where many Christians fail. So many of us cannot, or will not, go from being a Christian to becoming a disciple; a learner and follower of Christ. There is a great difference!

"Therefore go and make disciples of all nations, baptizing them in the name of the Father and of the Son and of the Holy Spirit, and teaching them to obey everything I have commanded you."
*Matthew 28:19-20a*

"And anyone who does not carry his cross and follow me cannot be my disciple." "In the same way, any of you who does not give up everything he has cannot be my disciple."
*Luke 14:26-27, 33*

"To the Jews who had believed him, Jesus said, 'If you hold to my teaching, you are really my disciples."
*John 8:31*

**DISCIPLESHIP IS A CHOICE!**

"Our Lord never insists upon obedience; He tells us very emphatically what we ought to do, but He never takes means to make us do it. We have to obey Him out of a oneness of spirit. That is why whenever Our Lord talked about discipleship, He prefaced it with an IF – you do not need to unless you like." (Oswald Chambers)

IF is defined as – in the event that; granting that; although possibly; even though. Our Lord has given us a choice; we have a free will.

As children, many of us played a game called "follow the leader." The leader - leads, guides and directs. A leader must have followers. The followers do whatever the leader commands. In the Body of Christ - Jesus is our leader. As believers we are His followers. We must do whatever He says. Amen?

"As Jesus was walking beside the Sea of Galilee, he saw two brothers, Simon called Peter and his brother, Andrew. They were casting a net into the lake, for they were fishermen. 'Come, follow me,' Jesus said, 'and I will make you fishers of men.' At once they left their nets and followed him."
*Matthew 4:18-20*

## BELOVED – WHO ARE YOU FOLLOWING TODAY?

## WHAT'S THE MEDIA BUZZ?

Within the past 30 years, or so, there has been a drastic moral declension in our society. Many of you know what I mean. You have witnessed the moral and spiritual degradation of our nation, and sadly our churches. Like our forefathers, we too have followed the way of Baal (lord, possessor) and have gone "whoring" after the gods of this nation. We have followed the dictates of our culture, society and harden hearts! Our "leaders" are leading us down a wicked and destructive path; and so many of us can only think of "Egypt".

"The Israelites said to them, 'If only we had died by the Lord's hand in Egypt! <u>There we</u> <u>sat around pots of meat and ate all the food we wanted</u>, but you have brought us out into the desert to starve this entire assembly to death."
*Exodus 16:3*

## QUESTION: DID THEY FORGET THEY WERE IN BONDAGE IN EGYPT AND HOW HARD THEY WERE FORCED TO WORK?

"They made their lives bitter with hard work in brick and mortar, and with all kinds of work in the fields; in all their hard labor the Egyptians used them ruthlessly."
*Exodus 1:14*

How soon we forget!

Today, the use of the television, radio, internet, cell phones, satellite, texting, I-pods, I-pads, twitting, etc. are definitely escalating. These great inventions and technologies have also become havens or cesspools of the most degrading forms of sexuality, sensuality and selfishness! Self is being exalted! Whatever self wants - self gets! The days that we now live in would put the days of Noah to shame! Beloved – this world has gone mad!

## QUESTION:HAVE YOU FORGOTTEN OUR MORALS FOR TODAY?

**"The Lord saw how great man's wickedness on the earth had become, and that every inclination of the thoughts of his heart was only evil all the time. The Lord was grieved that He had made man on the earth, and his heart was filled with pain."**
*Genesis 6:5-6*

**BELOVED – ARE YOU GRIEVING GOD'S HEART? REMEMBER – GOD SEES ALL!**

# CHAPTER TWO

:
●

"All Scripture is God-breathed and is useful for teaching,
rebuking, correcting in righteousness, so that the man of
God may be thoroughly equipped for every good work."
*II Timothy 3:16*

## WHAT IS OUR BIBLICAL FOUNDATION?

The book of Ephesians is an excellent tool in teaching the
Body of Christ. The central theme of this letter is God's
eternal purpose in establishing His Church and completing His
Body. It is a MUST study for all believers. The Apostle Paul, by
the Holy Spirit, outlines the position, practice and protection
of believers. It is the practice (habitual action or performance;
a habit or custom currently active or engaged in) of believers
that has come into great scrutiny today. It is also the behavior of
many believers today that has led to such corruption, shame and
disgrace in the Church of Jesus Christ.

Let's look at the Word of God (EPHESIANS – CHAPTER
4) and expound on the apostle's exhortation to his readers, and
to us today.

## IN RELATION TO OTHER BELIEVERS: EPHESIANS 4:1-6

"As a prisoner for the Lord, then, I urge you to live a life
worthy of the calling you have received. Be completely humble

and gentle; be patient bearing with one another in love. Make every effort to keep the unity of the Spirit through the bond of peace. There is one body and one Spirit - just as you were called - one Lord, one faith, one baptism. One God and Father of all, who is over all and through all and in all."

PROBLEM: We don't believe that as Christians we are one. We have allowed denominations, doctrines and dogmas to dissuade, divide and destroy the unity of believers.

FACT: All believers who have accepted Jesus Christ as their Savior are one! We will have different ideas, views, opinions, etc. But we must resist the ungodly notion that one particular set of people are better than others; that is demonic!

Our educational status, academic status, financial status, physical status or ecclesiastical status does not advance any of us into the Kingdom of God! We are translated into the Kingdom of God through His Son – Jesus Christ. God and His people are inseparable. His love is His law.

"Jesus replied; 'Love the Lord your God with all your heart and with all your soul and with all your mind.' This is the first and greatest commandment. And the second is like it: 'Love your neighbor as yourself.' All the Law and the Prophets hang on these two commandments."
Matthew 22:37-40

PRACTICE: There is an expectation of believers to promote the unity of the church (Body of Christ) through godly living and walking in love.

IN RELATION TO SPIRITUAL GIFTS: EPHESIANS 4:11-16

"It was He who gave some to be apostles, some to be prophets, some to be evangelists, and some to be pastors and teachers, to prepare God's people for works of service, so that the body of Christ may be built up until we all reach unity in the faith and in the knowledge of the Son of God and become mature, attaining to the whole measure of the fullness of Christ. Then we will no longer be infants, tossed back and forth by the waves, and blown here and there by every wind of teaching and by the cunning and craftiness of men in their deceitful scheming. Instead, speaking the truth in love, we will in all things grow up into him who is the Head, that is, Christ. From Him the whole body, joined and held together by every supporting ligament, grows and builds itself up in love, as each part does its work."

PROBLEM: We do not want anybody telling us what to do! We have either forgotten, or ignored the fact, that God set up the ministry, or hierarchy, in the Church of Jesus Christ. Today there is great dissension, discord and disunity in the Body of Christ.

FACT: Many believers are driven by positions and titles. There are too many self-appointed apostles, prophets, evangelists, pastors and teachers. Many are trying to function in these "God-appointed offices", whereby many have not been "called" to these offices, but may have these "gifts". THERE IS A GREAT DIFFERENCE! Some were called, some were sent and some just went!

"How, then, can they call on the one they have not believed in? And how can they believe in the one of whom they have not heard? And how can they hear without someone preaching to them? And how can they preach unless they are <u>sent</u>? As it is written, "How beautiful are the feet of those who bring good news!"
*Romans 10:14-15*

PRACTICE: As believers of Jesus Christ, we promote unity, maturity and service by NOT allowing spirits of jealousy, favoritism, false doctrines and pride to infest the Body of Christ. We must "walk in the spirit" at all times and maintain a spirit of humility.

## IN RELATION TO THE FORMER LIFE: EPHESIANS 4:22-24

"You were taught, with regard to your former way of life, to put off your old self, which is being corrupted by its deceitful desires; to be made new in the attitude of your minds, and to put on the new self, created to be like God in true righteousness and holiness."

PROBLEM: The old self is still on! Somehow we either don't know, or will not acknowledge, that the old is what we were <u>before</u> we were saved, and the new is the new life we <u>now</u> have in Christ.

FACT: There are many believers that still want to hold on to their old ways, i.e. bad attitudes, temperaments, criticisms and selfish desires. The enemy has deceived many believers into thinking that living a holy life is impossible; it just can't be done! Sadly, many have bought the lie!

"I have been crucified with Christ and I no longer live, but Christ lives in me. The life I live in the body, I live by faith in the Son of God, who loved me and gave Himself for me. I do not set aside the grace of God, for if righteousness could be gained through the law, Christ died for nothing!"
*Galatians 2:20-21*

PRACTICE: Crucifixion with Christ means death or separation from the reigning power of the old sinful life. It is the freedom to experience the power of the resurrection life of Christ by faith in God. There are some things that we do not need to resurrect. We must let them die! We must yield our entire spirit, soul and body to our Creator; He made us - He knows what's best!

## IN RELATION TO EVIL: EPHESIANS 5:8-13

"For you were once darkness, but now you are light in the Lord. Live as children of light (for the fruit of the light consists in all goodness, righteousness and truth) and find out what pleases the Lord. Have nothing to do with the fruitless deeds of darkness, but rather expose them. For it is shameful even to mention what the disobedient do in secret."

PROBLEM: Many believers do not, or will not, see evil as God sees it. Evil is often associated with the devil or something so wicked or detestable that many believers feel they cannot possibly be called evil. It doesn't apply to me! Evil is defined as – morally bad or wrong; wicked; causing ruin, injury or pain; harmful.

FACT: Far too many believers have determined to reside in the city of man. They want what the world wants; and behaves like the world also. What God calls evil - we have secularized to justify our cause. Sexual immorality is only immoral if you think that it is. Fornication is antiquated! "Everybody's doing it!" "What's so bad about it?" "God gave me these feelings!" Homosexuality is an alternative lifestyle. "Who are you to judge me?" "You can't help who you fall in love with!" "It's my body - I'll do with it what I want!" The statistics of the church mirror the statistics of the world: record number declensions in marriage; increased numbers of cohabitation, premarital sex, unwed mothers and fathers, pregnancies, etc. Immoralities of all kinds have inundated the world and the church! There are all kinds of corporate and ecclesiastical misdealing and embezzlements. Greed has corrupted many people, including believers.

"Therefore come out from among them and be separate says the Lord. Touch no unclean thing, and I will receive you. I will be a Father to you, and you will be my sons and daughters says the Lord Almighty."
*II Corinthians 6:17-18*

PRACTICE: As believers in Christ, our lives must be distinct; there must be a vast, grave and noticeable difference in the lifestyles and behaviors of God's people. By (believers) fostering the world's philosophies we, (believers) have "cheapened" the Word of God. There must be evidence (fruit) in the lives of all believers. Jesus says, "I AM the Vine, you are the branches".

(*see John -Chapter 15*) Holiness is not just a particular "dress code" or "set of rules", it is our sanctification (being set apart for a holy purpose); it is the LIFE of the believer. Beloved - "if the root is holy, so are the branches." *(Romans 11:16)*

## IN RELATION TO THE HOLY SPIRIT: EPHESIANS 5:18-21

"Do not get drunk on wine, which leads to debauchery. Instead, be filled with the Spirit. Speak to one another with psalms, hymns and spiritual songs. Sing and make music in your heart to the Lord, always giving thanks to God the Father for everything, in the name of our Lord Jesus Christ. Submit to one another out of reverence for Christ."

**PROBLEM:** Many believers are not filled with the Holy Spirit. Sadly, many in the Body of Christ do not acknowledge the Holy Spirit as being God. Many believers do not believe that drunkenness is sin! We are inundated with sipping saints! Beloved – that's another spirit!

**FACT:** There is a lack of understanding regarding who the Holy Spirit is and what His role is today. Many believers think that He is an "it"; a force of some kind and something that can be "caught" on Sundays. Being filled with the Holy Spirit is dependent upon our yieldedness to God's will. Also, the word "submit" is foreign; it is outdated and viewed as archaic! Many believers view submission as a sign of weakness or male dominance; thereby refusing to bow!

"And do not grieve the Holy Spirit of God, with whom you were sealed for the day of redemption."
*Ephesians 4:20*

**PRACTICE:** Get to know the Holy Spirit! He is a Person. He has feelings that can be grieved or pained by our sins, especially the sins of the tongue. Also, there should be a mutual respect for one another based on our reverence for God. To reverence God is to have reverential fear or "awe" of Him. We should have the "law of kindness" on our tongue and always be ready to defend our brothers and sisters honor, and also our God's!

## IN RELATION TO HOME LIFE: EPHESIANS 5:22-25

"Wives, submit to your husbands as to the Lord. For the husband is the head of the wife as Christ is the head of the church, His body, of which he is the Savior. Now as the church submits to Christ, so also wives should submit to their husbands in everything."

PROBLEM: There are many husbands who will not lead; and many wives who will not follow. Many fail to see the true biblical analogy of marriage - nor do we honor it. We think that marriage is just a piece of paper! We plan the wedding, but fail to plan for marriage – a lifetime commitment and a Godly covenant!

FACT: Many women, including believers, carry the spirit of independence. Many men, including believers, carry the spirit of pride. THE TWO BUMP HEADS! There are several female dominated organizations that have risen up against the Church of Jesus Christ. Many female believers have been deceived by their teachings. Many male believers have become comfortable, lazy-minded and have settled for mediocre living.

"For this reason a man will leave his father and mother and be united to his wife and the two will become one flesh. This is a profound mystery - but I am talking about Christ and the church."
*Ephesians 5:31*

PRACTICE: "Respect in marriage means ministering to your partner through listening, a loving embrace, a flexible mind and attitude, and a gracious spirit. It means looking past faults and differences, and seeing strengths and similarities. It means sharing concerns mutually instead of attempting to carry the load yourself." There must be an "interdependence"

- depending on each other - with Jesus Christ in the center of it all! "How can two walk together except they agree." *(Amos 3:3)*

**PROBLEM:** There is the absence of fathers in many homes. There are also multiple "fathering" in many homes. What household will the man/father maintain if he has multiple children? (children fathered by different women)

**FACT:** There are many believers, male and female, who will not bring their "temples" under the control of the Holy Spirit; there is no self-control! There are also many believers who have "decided" that sin is only sin IF you think that it is! These believers have "mixed" the world's value system with the godly values and principles of the Word of God, and have "created" a religion of their own; a religion - not a relationship. This is anti-God!

"Don't you know that you yourselves are God's temple and that God's Spirit lives in you? If anyone destroys God's temple, God will destroy him; for God's temple is sacred, and you are that temple."
*I Corinthians 3:16-17*

**PRACTICE:** We must "recognize" who we are in Christ Jesus! We do not have the power to keep ourselves; we are kept by the power of God! We must never attempt to see how close we can get to the world. We must view the world's system as an enemy of God.
*(see James 4:4-5)*

## IN RELATION TO HOME LIFE: EPHESIANS 6:1-4

"Children, obey your parents in the Lord, for this is right. 'Honor your father and mother' - which is the first commandment with a promise - 'that it may go well with you and that you may enjoy long life on the earth.' Fathers, do not exasperate your children; instead, bring them up in the training and instructions of the Lord."

**PROBLEM:** There are disobedient and rebellious children. There is a generation that has forgotten God! There are children that are torn between what they hear (about the love and goodness of God) in the church and what they see (ungodly and immoral parenting) in the home. There are "seeds" of immorality that were planted years ago; now it's harvest time!

FACT: Our society in inundated with psychiatrists, psychologists, counselors and ministers, etc. (That's O.K.!) However, as a church, we are failing to protect these innocent, precious children by not presenting the whole truth! Many churches are compromising and the leaders are hypocrites! Many of these children have grown up and become hard and callous adults who reject the Truth - God's Word!

Our schools have become the breeding grounds of obstinate, indifferent and irreverent youths. Is there any wonder why the number of teachers has declined? The home, of course, is the Christian acid test! Believers are exposed in the home. Family members, especially children who cannot speak out, witness the greatest hypocrisy right in the home. Is there any wonder that there is not a significant difference between believers and unbelievers? I KNOW - MANY ARE CARNAL!

"Brothers, I could not address you as spiritual but as worldly - mere infants in Christ. I gave you milk, not solid food, for you were not yet ready for it. Indeed, you are still not ready. You are still worldly."
*I Corinthians 3:1-3a*

PRACTICE: Believers of Jesus Christ must walk the talk! For many believers, living a carnal (fleshy) life is alright; it is appropriate for today. But it should not be! We are the light of the world! Everything exposed by the Light becomes visible. We must not allow the darkness of our past sins to overshadow the brightness of our "transformed" lives. Families do matter, especially to God!

"THE CHURCH IS NO STRONGER THAN THE
STRENGTH OF HER FAMILIES."

# CHAPTER THREE

$$\vdots$$

"But if serving the Lord seems undesirable to you, then choose for yourselves this day whom you will serve, whether the gods your forefathers served beyond the River, or the gods of the Amorites, in whose land you are living. But as for me and my household, we will serve the Lord."
*Joshua 24:20*

(THIS IS THE APEX AND THRUST OF THIS BOOK!)

THE CHURCH'S DILEMMA: WHAT CAN BELIEVERS OF THE GOSPEL OF JESUS CHRIST DO TO DISSUADE OR DISENCOURAGE UNGODLY BEHAVIOR - NAMELY SEXUAL IMMORALITY?

I am, by NO means, attempting to belittle, destroy or bash the Church of Jesus Christ. I am a member of the Body of Christ. But, we must take a stand against this "spirit" that has wreaked havoc in the masses! Every day we hear of another "soldier" who has gone AWOL! Where are the MPs? In our case - Messengers of Peace - who will bring these wounded, and sometimes misguided, soldiers home? Where are the seekers of Truth today?

Why are we so afraid to not only speak the Truth - but to live the Truth? Why is the world laughing and mocking the Church of Jesus Christ? WHAT IS SO FUNNY?

PROBLEM: THE CHURCH HAS GONE AFTER THE WORLD! There seems to be two extremes in the Body of Christ: there is an over-eagerness, anxiousness and a desperation to be married; to be completed. (Marriage is honorable!); then there are those believers who no longer view the marriage covenant as sacred or holy; they are "content" with living in sin, living a lie. Cohabitation is on the rise; the saints are not aware of its danger!

FACT: However, many believers, especially women, have gone after or fallen prey to men that do not love their God! (and vice versa) Many men are content with "casual" relationships; no commitment. Somehow women believe that they can <u>change</u> the men. THEY CANNOT! There seems to be an inability to wait on God; "He is too slow"; "He doesn't understand"; "I want it now!" These individuals simply do not believe God. They have allowed their natural feelings to dominate their spiritual senses. Many ministers and leaders will not take a stand in this matter. Many believers have compromised and abated the Word of God; allowances and excuses are being made for our sensual prowess ness. HENCE: divorce and sexual immorality is rampant in the Church of Jesus Christ! What happened to exercising self-control? It is a fruit of the Spirit - isn't it? (see *Galatians 5:22*) I, personally, have a question that truly amazes, yet annoys my spirit: How can anyone have a spouse and a fiancé' (two different individuals) - at the same time? HELP US LORD!

"Do not be yoked together with unbelievers. For what do righteousness and wickedness have in common? Or what fellowship can light have with darkness? What harmony is there between Christ and Belial? What does a believer have in common with an unbeliever? What agreement is there between the temple of God and idols? As God has said: I will live with them and walk among them, and I will be their God, and they will be my people."
*II Corinthians 6:14-16*

This injunction applies to marriage, business, to ecclesiastical (church folks) and to intimate personal relationships.

PRACTICE: ALL believers must adhere to the teachings of scripture. The Word of God is the Word of God! He is speaking to His children, those who are called by His Name. God has given us His Holy Spirit; God lives in us! Believers often quote, "I can do everything through Him who gives me strength." (see *Philippians 4:13* ) Yet, in a moment of weakness we tend to forget, or fail to appropriate, His Word. We forget that in every temptation, God makes a way of escape!

"No temptation has seized you except what is common to man. And God is faithful; He will not let you be tempted beyond what you can bear. But when you are tempted, He will also provide a way out so that you can stand up under it."
*I Corinthians 10:13*

Beloved – God has your back, your front, your sides, your top and your bottom. He is covering you with Himself! God has given us commandments (rules to live by). These are not suggestions or options! We cannot pick and choose; we must obey them all! God is not trying to make our lives miserable. Jesus Christ came that we might have life, and that more abundantly. (*see John 10:10b*)

If God is saying NO to something that we are feeling anxious about - we must remember what the Word says, wait for direction from the Word and appropriate (obey) His Word:

"Do not be anxious about anything, but in everything, by prayer and petition, with thanksgiving, present your requests to God. And the peace of God, which transcends all understanding will guard your hearts and your minds in Christ Jesus."
*Philippians 4:6-7*

## LEARN TO DISCERN!

O.K. - this foundation (or digression) was inserted to set forth the Word of God as the ONLY true standard, principle, law, precept, etc. God's Word is His Word!

However, there is a "strange" spirit in the air. Let's first look at the definition of strange: unusual, peculiar, eccentric, unfamiliar, alien, not at ease, out of one's element.

What I mean by a strange spirit is this: There is a teaching, a doctrine, and/or gospel that is NOT the truth. IT IS A LIE! Oh yes (you are thinking) there are many - and there are! But as we see in *II Timothy 3:1-17* (yes - read it!) these are perilous/terrible times. Many people have taken "false prophets" to heart. These false prophets are spreading propaganda that attacks the Word of God. Sadly, there are many believers who have fallen prey, become victimized, seduced and deceived by these leaders and their teachings. My spirit is not at ease with this great lie. What about yours? IT'S TIME TO CRY OUT!

II Peter, Chapter 2 - tells of the denunciation of false teachers. PEOPLE -READ IT OVER AND OVER UNTIL IT GETS IN YOUR SPIRIT! This is exactly where we are today - right now. It is as if Apostle Peter is speaking to us today. Many of us are failing to heed these warnings. We have found "teachers" to guide us and we are now relishing on these new (but not so new) teachings, especially the teachings regarding sexuality and marriage.

"The Spirit clearly says that in later times some will abandon the faith and follow deceiving spirits and things taught by demons. Such teachings come through hypocritical liars, whose consciences have been seared as with a hot iron. They forbid people to marry and order them to abstain from certain foods, which God created with thanksgiving by those who believe and know the truth."
*I Timothy 4:1-3*

The Apostle Paul has some more words to say to us as well: "I am astonished that you are so quickly deserting the one who called you by the grace of Christ and are running to a <u>different</u> gospel - which is no gospel at all. Evidently some people are throwing you into confusion and are trying to pervert the gospel of Christ. But even if we or an angel from heaven should preach a gospel other than the one we preached to you, let him be eternally condemned. As we have already said, so now I say again. If anybody is preaching to you a gospel other than what you accepted, let him be eternally condemned!"
*Galatians 1:6-8*

What we must understand is this - a half truth is a whole lie! It is a web of deception that is being woven into the very fabric of our churches, families and world. As many of us know - there are multitudinous "religions" in our world today. However, there is only one religion (which is not a religion - but a relationship) in which its followers bow (come under the supreme authority) to its leader. Christianity says that Christ is King (God); other religions say that you (the person) are a god. Christianity acknowledges the sovereign rule of God over one's entire life; religion says that you design your own life - you rule your own roost; there are no absolutes - you are it! Religion has taken a front seat in the heart of many today. Many are on a "spiritual quest" for truth – AND THE ENEMY LIES TO THEM!

Could it be that millions are "seeking" to fill the void in their hearts? That God-ordained void? But instead of "submitting" to the God of the Universe these religionists or spiritualists are worshiping the Universe. They want to worship the Universe of God - but are refusing to worship the God of the Universe. In essence, they want the things of God - minus God. That is the "new" teaching of today; it is a false teaching. IT IS AN OLD LIE!

"When you recognize the unconsciousness in you, that which makes the recognition possible is the arising consciousness, is awakening. You cannot fight against the ego and win, just as you cannot fight against darkness. The light of consciousness is all that is necessary. You are the light." Eckhart Tolle – A New World Order.

"The eye is the lamp of the body. If your eyes are good, your whole body will be full of light. But if your eyes are bad, your whole body will be full of darkness. If then the light within you is darkness, how great is that darkness!" Jesus Christ – The Word of God.
*Matthew 6:22-23*

So - what does this "strange" spirit have to do with you and I? It is being perceived by many Christians/believers as being God's Truth. It does not require a separation from the world or a renouncing of sin, because THERE IS NO SIN! GOD HELP US! Sin is subjective (proceeding from personal idiosyncrasy or individuality; not impartial or literal) But sin is more that that - it is serious business. It separates the creation (human beings) from the Creator (Almighty God). It took Jesus Christ to recon-cile (bridge the gap) from fallen man - back to God due to our sin. It cost Him his life- in order that we would gain life. Can we all say -THANK YOU JESUS? More importantly – can we thank Him with our lives? And possibly help someone else?

"My brothers if one of you should wander from the truth and someone should bring him back, remember this: WHOEVER turns a sinner from the error of his way will save him from death and cover a multitude of sins."
*James 5:19*

41

# CHAPTER FOUR

•
•
•

"Finally, be strong in the Lord and in His mighty power. Put
on the full armor of God so that you can take your stand
against the devil's schemes. For our struggle is not against
flesh and blood, but against the rulers, against the authorities,
against the powers of this dark world and against the
spiritual forces of evil in the heavenly realms."
*Ephesians 6:10-12*

## NOW TO THE CRUX!

P.K.'s (preacher's kids) seem to live an exceptionally hard
life. I have seen the rise and fall of many preachers' kids.
(Trust me - I know!) They are often subjected to the scrutiny
of many well-meaning (and not so well-meaning) Christians.
There are great "expectations" from the family and the church
about how the preacher's kids should behave. (YOU WOULD
THINK THAT THEY SHOULD KNOW BETTER!) I believe
that these expectations put many, if not most, of the preacher's
kids in jeopardy. They cannot, or will not, attempt to meet such
expectations; many have given up trying. These expectations
also place preachers in a "micro-management" role. They must
now "watch" their children to ensure that the expectations of
others are met; then add their own - just in case!

Ministers of the Gospel: Apostles, Prophets, Evangelists,
Pastors, Teachers, Elders, Bishops, Deacons, Deaconess', etc.

are on the enemy's "hit list"; and so are their families. This also includes ANYONE who wants to live godly. Anyone that God has raised up to be an orator of the Gospel - is open season for the devil. That includes you beloved!

When the enemy cannot penetrate your shield of faith - he retreats to your camp ground. He knows that everyone is NOT watching and praying. He knows that every chain has a weak link, and he goes after it. He pulls and tugs relentlessly until the chain snaps! He then walks away thinking to himself, "mission accomplished". And just what was his mission? Jesus said it best in *John 10:10a*, "the thief comes but for to kill, steal and destroy." In essence, he comes to kill your joy (You're just too happy!); to steal your message (The gospel is good news!) and to destroy your life. (All that God ordained for you!) He uses sin, yours or your family members, to silence the Word of God. He tempts one to sin, then comes right back and accuses that very one of the sin he tempted them to commit. What a snake! Jesus tells us that the devil is a liar and the father of lies. (*see John 8:44.*) In essence - the first lie that was ever told was committed by the devil; he invented lies. Jesus also tells us in *John 10:10b*, "I have come that they may have life, and have it to the full." What a consolation! Thank you Jesus!

It takes a sold-out soul to experience the power, authority and anointing of God. (As believers, we all have the power, authority and anointing.) But there are those who have been progressively sanctified. (There are stages of sanctification. Read and study *I Corinthians 6:11.*) There are those who are truly abiding in Christ. (*see John 15*) There are also those that are struggling everyday to not only please God - but the people of God. PEOPLE PLEASERS! We all know them; maybe you are one! I was one also.

What I personally love about the Word of God is its honesty. The Bible is brutally honest! God did not leave anything out. He has shown us the good, the bad and the ugly. In spite of all the unfaithfulness of men and women - God remains faithful. In spite of the all the untrustworthiness of men and women - God remains trustworthy. In spite of all the lies of men and women - God remains true. His Word declares-

"Let God be true and every man a liar...So that you may be proved right when you speak and prevail when you judge."
*Romans 3:4*

---

## DO WE PREPARE FOR MARRIAGE?

God is a righteous Judge and He always does what is right. Believers have a covenant with God. This covenant is often liken to a marriage. For many today, it is a fight to stay married!

---

Now, let's continue to look at the Word of God as it relates to believers in terms of marriage. God likens the church (believers) to the BRIDE OF CHRIST.

"Husbands, love your wives, just as Christ loved the church and gave himself up for her to make her holy, cleansing her by the washing with water through the word, and to present her to himself as a radiant church, without stain or wrinkle or any other blemish, but holy and blameless."
*Ephesians 5:25-27*

"Let us rejoice and be glad and give him glory! For the wedding of the Lamb has come, and his bride has made herself ready."
*Revelation 19:7*

"I saw the Holy City, the new Jerusalem, coming down out of heaven from God, prepared as a bride beautifully dressed for her husband....One of the seven angels who had the seven bowls full of the seven last plagues came and said to me, "Come, I will show you the bride, the wife of the Lamb."
*Revelation 21:2, 9*

## QUESTION: WHAT COMES TO MIND WHEN YOU THINK OF A BRIDE?

The Oxford Dictionary defines bride as - a woman on her wedding day and for some time before and after is. Wedding is defined as - a marriage ceremony (considered by itself or with the associated celebration). To wed means to join in marriage, to unite, obstinately attached or devoted.

It is a sad, yet true, commentary that many of us will not believe the Bible; but we will believe the dictionary! So, the dictionary says what God has already said! But God takes it further.

"Marriage should be honored by all, and the marriage bed kept pure, for God will judge the adulterer and all the sexually immoral."
*Hebrews 13:4*

"Marriage is honorable in all, and the bed undefiled, but whoremongers and adulterers God will judge."
*King James Version – Hebrews 13:4*

An adulterer is a married person who is having a sexual relationship with someone other than his/her spouse. So - who is a whoremonger? I TOLD YOU THAT THE WORD OF GOD IS HONEST!

Because of our rebellious spirit and our love for this world's system - we now say – "marriage should be whatever you want it to be." "A piece of paper cannot and does not validate a "loving" union." "As long as you love someone, it's alright to have sex with them." "God understands; He loves me." "God does not judge me!"

In essence - we have tried to re-write the Bible. We have tried to make it "fit" our immoral lifestyles. We have huffed our finite and carnal selves up in the face of God. We have openly declared, 'TO HELL WITH YOUR WORD - WE HAVE OUR OWN!' Sadly, many believers have responded with an arousing - AMEN! Church - what a dilemma! What an apostasy! What a shame and disgrace! Beloved – who are you espoused to? Do you have "irreconcilable differences" with the Lord? Are you ready for a divorce? God hates divorce!

The truth of the matter is - there is no more shame and disgrace to our open immorality. We are now proud and boastful. We have a peacock strut, and we are proud of it- thank you! The Church of Jesus Christ has gotten comfortable (relaxed, at ease, free from discomfort, having an adequate standard of living, having an easy conscience). And why not? After all - we have been hearing, for over 2,000 years, that Jesus Christ is coming back. Where is He? Some have gone so far as to say that He does not exist. Many believers have taken the road of Demas.

"For Demas has forsaken me, having loved this present world."
*II Timothy 4:10a*

By the way - did you know that Demas' name means "popular" (liked or admired by many people or by a specified group). Uh-oh - as believers we must be careful, watchful and prayerful. When the world (the devil's system) welcomes you as a friend - you're now an enemy of God!

"Ye adulterers and adulteresses, know ye not that the friendship of the world is enmity with God? Whosoever therefore will be a friend of the world IS the enemy of God."
*James 4:4 King James Version*

The term adulterers and adulteresses is symbolic language for unfaithful creatures. In essence - one has left his marriage covenant, with God, and has gone whoring after the things of the world. As believers we cannot lower God's standards for our lives; God certainly will not lower His. We seem to want to lower the bar; we make statements such as; 'nobody can live holy', 'everybody is doing it', 'everybody got something that they are struggling with', 'if it ain't one thing, it's another.' We make any excuse to sin against God! We blame our flesh - "the spirit is willing but the flesh is weak" - <u>in every instance</u>.

But wait Church! Where is our discernment; knowing good from evil? What about the Holy Spirit? What exactly is His purpose? The greatest misuse of power today is the non-use of the Holy Spirit. We simply do not believe, trust or rely on the power of God to rescue us out of every situation!

"No temptation has seized you except what is common to man. And God is faithful; he will not let you be attempted beyond what you can bear. But when you are tempted, he will also provide a way out so that you can stand up under it."
*I Corinthians 10:13*

On a daily basis, the Holy Spirit is grieved by the words that we speak. We speak a plethora of "I cannots" to His loving invitation - "Come to me all you who are weary and heavy laden." Yet, with the same breath, and sometimes even in the same sentence, we say, "I can do all things through Christ who strengthens me." *(KJV)* BUT (nevertheless, however, on the other hand, except) I AM STILL HUMAN! We are so at home in this piece of dust. We make provisions for this decaying matter, i.e. jobs, cars, houses, makeovers, cosmetology, eating at the finest restaurants, lounging at the best clubs, etc., etc. - not realizing that this frame will give away and return back to the earth from whence is came. PLEASE - we should, and must, take care of our bodies - but we are not to idolize them! We are to present our bodies as living sacrifices unto the Lord.

"Therefore, I urge you, brothers, in view of God's mercy, to offer your bodies as living sacrifices, holy and pleasing to God - this is your spiritual act of worship. Do not conform any longer to the pattern of this world, but be transformed by the renewing of your mind. Then you will be able to test and approve what God's will is - his good, pleasing and perfect will."
*Romans 12:1-2*

Beloved -what provisions have you made for God's temple? Is your temple (body) righteous and sanctified? Do you offer the best or seek to be the best? I know - the flesh is "showy" and the Spirit is invisible. But then - many believers are entertainers - they are performance driven. APPLAUSE! APPLAUSE!

The bottom line is that we are in a war! We are battling for ourselves, our families, our churches, our cities, our nations and our world. We are often confused about who the "real" enemy is; we are fighting amongst ourselves; we are walking in deception; we are not standing on the word of God!

"For though we live in the world, we do not wage war as the world does. The weapons we fight with are not the weapons of the world. On the contrary, they have divine power to demolish strongholds. We demolish arguments and every pretension that sets itself up against the knowledge of God, and we take captive every thought to make it obedient to Christ."
*II Corinthians 10:4-5*

# CHAPTER FIVE

$\vdots$

"When God gets us alone by affliction, heartbreak, or temptation, by disappointment, sickness, or by thwarted affection, by
a broken friendship, or by a new friendship – when He gets us
absolutely alone, and we are dumbfounded, and cannot ask
one question, then He begins to expound."
Oswald Chambers

When I started this writing - I thought that I would be
saying a few words about sexual immorality. I wanted
so much to convey the sadness and heartache of how many
believers, especially the Ministers of the Gospel and P.K.'s, have
fallen prey to the "lust" of the flesh. As you can see - the Lord
has done so much more. He has laid the foundation, or standard,
of holiness. He has spoken via His Word on what He expects
believers to be, and how believers should live. He has also given
believers a mandate to follow. He asks some very poignant questions, especially to those that minister to others.

"You then, who teach others, do you not teach yourselves? You
who preach against stealing, do you steal? You who say that
people should not commit adultery, do you commit adultery? You
who abhor idols, do you rob temples? You who brag about the
law, do you dishonor God by breaking the law? As it is written;
God's name is blasphemed among the Gentiles because of you."
*Romans 2:21-24*

These questions should stir our hearts. There is a great hypocrisy noted in the Church of Jesus Christ. There are many noted men and women of God - who talk the talk but do not walk the walk! This "spirit" of hypocrisy is spreading like wildfire in the Church. There are many moral and religious people who glory in their spiritual positions, yet their lives do not reflect the Glory of God. This behavior has caused many unbelievers to remain UNBELIEVERS!

In stating these scriptures (noted above) the Apostle Paul presented the Jews with their own laws, then turned the tables on them. He exposed the hypocrisy of their hearts. The Jews, questioned, were guilty of doing these things after telling others not to do them. The failure of the Jew makes him culpable because of privileges he had in the law and the promises of God. He could and should have become a guide and light to those in darkness.

An honest Jew would have to respond to Apostle Paul's questions by admitting his guilt and hypocrisy. Paul did not use his own authority, as an Apostle, to condemn the Jews but quoted scripture; He used God's Word. The Jews' hypocrisy dishonored God and caused Gentiles to blaspheme God.

"And now what do I have here?" declares the Lord. "For my people have been taken away for nothing, and those who rule them mock," declares the Lord. "And all day long my name is constantly blasphemed."
*Isaiah 52:5*

Do you see the Church's dilemmas of today? The Jews are symbolic of the leadership of the Church (those who preach and teach the Word of God). These questions should bring us to humility. They should burn in our hearts and minds, night and day. There should be a holy cry for God's Truth. Our failure, to honor God's Word, also makes us culpable because of our relationship to Jesus Christ. These noted questions should be answered in the affirmative. What do you say? I say that we need the Holy Spirit's help right now!

**"Not many of you should presume to be teachers, my brothers, because you know that we who teach will be judged more strictly."**
*James 3:1*

Also, like the Apostle Paul, we too must use the Word of God to present truth. The hypocrisy of believers today has also dishonored God and caused unbelievers to blaspheme our Lord. One of the greatest, and most visible, sins committed in the Church of Jesus Christ is sexual immorality. It is also the sin that dishonors, not only God, but our own bodies.

**"Flee from sexual immorality. All other sins a man commits are outside his body, but he who sins sexually sins against his own body. Do you not know that your body is a temple of the Holy Spirit, who is in you, whom you have received from God?"**
*I Corinthians 6:18-19*

**"We should not commit sexual immorality, as some of them did-and in one day twenty-three thousand of them died."**
*I Corinthians 10:8*

**"But among you there must not be even a hint of sexual immorality, or of any kind of impurity, or of greed, because these are improper for God's holy people."**
*Ephesians 5:3*

**THE APOSTLE IS SPEAKING TO BELIEVERS! ARE YOU CRYING YET?**

Somehow, many believers today do not believe (no pun intended) that this Word of God applies to them. But it does! It is still applicable to believers today - as it was in the Apostle's day. The Word of God declares that God does not change; people do.

Personally, I take a strong stance against sexual immorality. I was once bound by this demon and was enslaved to its passions. Jesus Christ set me free! I know the struggles that believers face when desiring to be free. I know the vacillations of the heart and mind when one is wrestling with the enemy. I also know the "pleasure" of sexual sin - which only lasts for a season. There are many "sins" that are wreaking havoc in the Church of Jesus Christ; none of us are immune to its' possibilities. The Apostle Paul experienced a struggle with sin, as well. <u>(not necessarily sexual sin, but this is applicable</u>)

"I know that nothing good lives in me, that is, in my sinful nature. For I have the desire to do what is good, but I cannot carry it out. For what I do is not the good that I want to do; no, the evil I do not want to do – this I keep on doing. Now if I do what I do not want to do, it is no longer I who do it, but it is sin living in me that does it."
*Romans 7:18-20*

Yet, primarily it is sexual sin that is on the forefront! This world's system pays, literally, millions of dollars to sell us this immorality. The enemy glamorizes and glorifies these demonic acts. Sadly, not only the world has bought this propaganda, but so has the church. Believers are compromising and making numerous excuses for what is now called a "lifestyle". Sin is no longer noted to characterize one's "choices". SEX SELLS - PERIOD! Where there is a demand there will always be a supply. As a nation of immoral people, there is an exorbitant demand! Look at the influx of pornography today! We have opened our homes to the filth of the world; and many of us are loving it!

Due to the Church's laxity and compromising behavior these spirits of sexual immorality have established "strongholds" in the hearts and minds of many believers. From the pulpit to the pew - many believers have fallen prey to this "animal". Sexual immorality has single-handedly "knocked-out" many preachers and parishioners; some have never recuperated. Why? Why have many believers who have been baptized into the Body of Christ - by the Holy Spirit - fallen prey to sexual immorality? DESIRE!

"But each one is tempted when, by his own evil desire, he is dragged away and enticed. Then after desire, has conceived, it gives birth to sin; and sin, when it is full-grown, gives birth to death."
*James 1:14-15*

This epistle of James was written to believers! Many people today, including believers, love to say, "the devil made me do it." It is an easy cop-out! Most of us will NOT take responsibility for our actions. Temptations, of all sorts, come to all of us. The temptations are not sin; it is the yielding to them! The source of temptation is from within a person; his/her own evil desire, lust or inner craving. Desire is defined as – to wish or long for; sexual appetite, passion.

Sin does not force itself on the UNWILLING. We choose sin because it "appears" to be attractive, and most of us only see the present situation and not the future consequence. Sin is like an addiction – the habit takes over! The person is dragged away and enticed; like bait for a fish – it lures – then snaps them up! Temptation begins with an evil (morally bad or wrong; causing ruin, injury, pain; harmful) thought. The thought becomes sin when one dwells on it. It is then allowed to become an action. "Temptations are often the combination of a real need and a possible doubt that creates an inappropriate desire." The wrong response to temptation will result in spiritual poverty and ultimately death.

"For if you live according to the sinful nature, you will die; but if by the Spirit you put to death the misdeeds of the body, you will live."
*Romans 8:13*

**BELOVED – KILL IT OR IT WILL KILL YOU! DON'T BE DECEIVED!**

We must learn to resist all evil temptations. Resist means to – withstand the action or effect of; stop the course or progress of; abstain from (pleasure, temptation, etc.); refuse to comply with). Joseph, a young and handsome man, knew how to resist temptation – HE RAN!

"One day he went into the house to attend his duties, and none of the household servants was inside. She (*Potiphar's wife*) caught him by his cloak and said, "Come to bed with me!" But he left his cloak in her hand and ran out of the house."
*Genesis 39:11-12 (author's italics)*

Joseph could have possibly "gotten away" with this sin. Mrs. Potiphar surely would not have told her husband; she would have continued to seduce this young and handsome man of God. Mr. Potiphar may never had known. But God knew; and so did Joseph. He was not willing to "bow" to the prowess of the King's wife, thereby disobeying his God. Joseph loved God more than fleshy desires! Sin is a choice! Beloved – what are you choosing today? Can you still run? TAKE A STAND!

"Therefore submit to God. Resist the devil and he will flee from you. Draw near to God and He will draw near to you."
*James 4:7-8*

CAUTION TO BELIEVERS!

We are ALL capable of sin. We must be accountable to God, our leadership and the Body of Christ. We are a puzzle; connected to each other. One missing piece renders the puzzle incomplete. No one is immune to this beast! And we all need one another!

"If anyone thinks he is something when he is nothing, he deceives himself."
*Galatians 6:3*

## IF YOU THINK YOU STAND – TAKE HEED LEST YOU FALL!
## "WHAT CAN WASH AWAY MY SIN? NOTHING BUT THE BLOOD OF JESUS!"

**"For it pleased the Father that in Him all the fullness should dwell, and by Him to reconcile all things to Himself, by Him, whether things on earth or things in heaven, having made peace through the blood of His cross. And you, who once were alienated and enemies in your mind by wicked works, yet now He has reconciled in the body of His flesh through death, to present you holy, and blameless, and irreproachable in His sight."**
*Colossians 1:19-22*

Many believers have not appropriated the power of the cross of Jesus Christ; the atoning blood of Jesus Christ and the resurrected power of Jesus Christ to their everyday lives. The flesh has gotten out of control! IT MUST BE CRUCIFIED! If we are not submitting, yielding and surrendering our lives to the total control of the Holy Spirit, on a daily basis, we will continue to struggle and be defeated by the flesh. We must know that we are playing with fire, and getting burned. Believer – the flesh knows how to fight!

There are many reasons for the believer's demise: ignorance of the Word of God, a lack of spiritual maturity, a lack of spiritual discernment, a misunderstanding of the Word of God, not appropriating God's Word to every situation and/or problem, not being filled with the Holy Spirit, etc. The list is inexhaustive! Yet whatever the reason(s) for the believer's declension - many are living a lie. This hypocrisy dishonors God and brings a shame and reproach to His Holy Name.

On the other hand - many unbelievers have reasoned: Why should we honor God - when His children (the church) do not follow him? Why should we go to church -when His children, who do go to church, commit the same sins that we do? Why should we believe that the Bible is the Word of God - when His children don't obey it? Why should we get married - when His children are co-habiting? Why should we abstain from pre-marital sex or sexual sin - when His children are having babies out of wedlock every day? Why should we tell the truth - when His children are liars?

## BELIEVER - DO YOU CARE TO ANSWER?

I would say that these unbelievers have good reasons NOT to become believers in Christ (if it were left up to many Christians). BUT IT IS NOT! Jesus Christ is the epitome of love and truth - yet many of His followers are questionable. Why? Primarily because Jesus is not Lord of the believer's life. He does not rule and reign. He has not been allowed to sit on the throne of their hearts. These believer's sins have dethroned the King of Kings and Lord of Lords. Jesus has been relegated to a man; a mere human being. By this relegation – many believers think that they do not have to obey Him, honor Him, esteem Him or follow Him. His words are no different than any of the other so-called prophets, gurus or spiritists of today. THEY DON'T SEE THE DIFFERENCE!

Now this may sound facetious, but it's true. Many believers will never verbalize these truths; but on a daily basis they will live them out. This, Church of Jesus Christ, is OUR hypocrisy. It is the "family" secret; outsiders (unbelievers) are not allowed to judge us. We are the Church - we can sin! Sadly, these same believers refuse to be disciplined, admonished or rebuked by the leadership of the Church; even if the leadership is in accord with the Word of God. There is a body of rebellious believers. What an oxymoron!

I have witnessed this catastrophe, this rebellion and this ungodliness first hand. There are some believers (and unbelievers) who will rise up and confront you to your face. They will say to you: 'Who do you think you are? Who are you to judge me? I am a Christian just like you! You must think that you are holier than thou! You are not my Savior! This is my life! God loves me just as much as He loves you!' And so on and on.

I don't have a problem with most of these people; I know where they are coming from. I can see the demons rising up in them. I can exercise my God-given authority over them (the demons)! However, it is the passive-aggressive believers that I take exception with; they are the Judas' of our day. They will eat with you, walk with you and stab you in the back; all the while <u>professing</u> to be a follower of Christ. They will sell you out with the kiss of death. I pray for a discerning spirit; that all believers may know good from evil and truth from error. Now, isn't it time to cry out?

The Word of God SHOULD transform us (make a thorough or dramatic change in the form, outward appearance, character, etc.) As believers we should exemplify Christ. The Word works. God does not lie! Yet hard or gentle, long or short, in season or out of season - as the preacher preaches - the Word of God will, and sometimes does, fall on deaf ears. If the preacher preached exactly WHAT the people wanted, WHEN the people wanted and HOW they wanted it - we would have a unified Church. People would come to Church in droves. There would not be any conviction; only compromise. BUT WE WOULD BE HAVING CHURCH! So we think. Beloved – it's time for believers to BE the Church!

There would, however, not be any ministry of the Holy Spirit. Jesus tells us the purpose of the Holy Spirit coming into the world.

"When He comes, He will <u>convict</u> the world of guilt in regard to sin and righteousness and judgment: in regard to sin, because men do not believe in me; in regard to righteousness, because I am going to the Father, where you can see me no longer, and in regard to judgment, because the prince of this world now stands condemned."
*John 16:8-11*

In essence, the Holy Spirit - through Apostles, Prophets, Evangelists, Pastors and Teachers, etc. will convict the world. To convict means to set forth the truth of the gospel in such a clear light that men/women are able to ACCEPT or REJECT it intelligently; to convince men/women of the truthfulness of the gospel. The greatest, and basic, sin is UNBELIEF! Jesus Christ triumphed over Satan (the prince of this world); serving notice on unbelievers of their judgment to come. OH YES - there is a judgment to come! There is also a gross misunderstanding of God's Word, and His messengers. Today there are many that believe that preaching the Word of God is foolishness.

"For since in the wisdom of God the world through its wisdom did not know him, God was pleased through the foolishness of what was preached to save those who believe."
*I Corinthians 1:21*

## CAUTION TO UNBELIEVERS!

Even though there may be hypocrites in the Church - God does not excuse your intelligent decision to REJECT His Only Begotten Son - Jesus; The Savior of the World. You will also have to give an account of the deeds done in your body. You are in need of a Savior. Jesus Christ is the Savior. You must accept Him as Your Savior and Lord. You must repent! (Have a change of heart and mind.)

"Jesus said to him, "I am the way, the truth, and the life. No one comes to the Father except through Me."
*John 14:6*

"Behold, I am coming soon! My reward is with me, and I will give to everyone according to what he has done. I am the Alpha and Omega, the First and the Last, the Beginning and the End."
*Revelation 22:12-13*

## GLORY GLORY – END OF STORY!

# CHAPTER SIX

. . .

"And I also say to you that you are Peter, and on this rock
I will build My church, and the gates of Hell
not prevail against it."
Matthew 16:18

## HELP US LORD!

I often sit and talk with the Father about His Church. I wonder, out loud, what will happen to this Body of believers? I literally cry and weep - gasping for answers. My questions to my Father are: "What can I do Lord? How can I help? How can I make a difference? What can the believers do to stop this domino effect? How can we stop this avalanche of sin?" My heart truly aches for the Body of Christ! I have children (sons) and these "spirits" of the world has infiltrated my camp!

I, however, am not immune to these spirits of the world. For three years I walked in a backslidden condition; I strayed from the teachings of God. I went back into the world. The Bible says:

"As a dog returns to its vomit, so a fool repeats his folly."
*Proverbs 26:11*

It further states:

"Of them the proverbs are true: "A dog returns to its vomit", and," A sow that is washed goes back to her wallowing in the mud."
*II Peter 2:22*

Anyone that has been in a backslidden condition can attest to the truths of these words. It is horrific! I walked in fear every day. I feared that I would die and not go to heaven. I feared that God would punish me for turning my back on Him. I feared that I would never "make it up" to God. I feared for my life and the lives of my family. But after three years of hell - this prodigal came home! And like the prodigal son, in *Luke- Chapter 15*, the Father welcomed me home. PRAISE GOD! He did not berate, belittle or judge me. He did not condemn or scold me. He simply impressed upon my heart how much He loved me! As much as I wanted to continue to explain my disobedience - He held me - like a tender mother and a strong father- in His loving arms and forgave me. For a while, I could not forgive myself. I thought that I should have had a long period of time to allow the punishment to take place. BUT GOD! His love and forgiveness is so special, and so right on time. I knew that God had thrown my sins into the "sea of forgetfulness"; never to remember them anymore!

Of course, with any sin, there must be repentance (having a change of heart and mind). I confessed my sin and my Father was faithful and just to forgive me and cleanse me from all unrighteousness. *(see I John 1:9)* Sin also has consequences (the result or effect of an action or condition). Because of my choices I had to reap what I had sown. But God was with me.

"Do not be deceived, God is not mocked; for whatever a man sows, that he will also reap."
*Galatians 6:7*

I also knew that I had to maintain my deliverance by living a holy life and not being idle.

Jesus said:

**"When an evil spirit comes out of a man, it goes through arid places seeking rest and does not find it. Then it says, 'I will return to the house I left.' When it arrives, it finds the house unoccupied, swept clean and put in order. Then it goes and takes with it seven other spirits more wicked than itself, and they go in and live there. The final condition of that man is worse than the first."**
*Matthew 12:43-44*

I wholeheartedly believed that these scriptures applied to me, and to so many others. When I gave my life to the Lord, I was ecstatic, elated, overjoyed - the words are endless! I was zealous for God. I read the Word of God night and day. I told others about Him. I wasn't ashamed of my conversion. I was happy to be saved. Then my balloon began to dissipate; to lose air. I began to become confused. I listened to well-meaning, <u>and not so well-meaning</u>, Christians. There were those that wanted to "set me straight". I was given more rules and regulations than the House of Congress! There were more of the "you can not's", than the "you can's". Finally, I just said to myself - "I can't do this; I can't live a holy life" - and back to the world I went.

I got involved with things that I didn't even do as an unbeliever! My life was a restless evil. I felt that I did not fit in with the world or with the Church; I felt so out of place any and everywhere I went. The enemy would impress upon my heart to "end it". He would tell me that nobody understood what I was going through; that I had tried to be holy - and that was enough. BUT GOD! God was, and is, Faithful! I remember talking to God many nights. There were many midnight hours of crying and feeling sorry for my sins. I felt immobilized, unable to get back on track; frozen in sin, self and satanic pleasures. You see, I really did love the company that I kept; unsaved family members and friends. My mind would wander and I would wonder out loud - What if I do something wrong? What if I fail? What if - what if - what if?

I remember pitying myself for not being able to live a holy life. I said to God, "just forget about me, don't speak to me anymore, I don't deserve you even listening to me." But God reminded me of a heartfelt prayer that I had prayed right after my conversion. I said to the Lord, "Father, if I ever go back into the world, please make it so hard for me - that I cannot stay in the world." AND HE ANSWERED THAT HEARTFELT PRAYER! I WAS MISERABLE IN MY SIN! When I began to understand that God was answering my prayer - I rejoiced! I thanked God! All of a sudden I knew what was happening; I couldn't stay in the world; the world could not hold me because God was holding me. PRAISE GOD! So- I returned to my God and He abundantly pardoned me! BLESS GOD!

What about you beloved? Where are you today on your spiritual journey? Maybe you have made some unplanned stops; maybe you have been sidetracked, or have taken a detour. Let me help you today, by telling you that it is time to get back on track, to rise up and get going! Don't waste precious time and energy looking back - go forward in Jesus' Name! The Father is waiting for you to come home! And the Body of Christ needs you!

So beloved - yes I understand the dilemma that so many believers are facing today. I understand the struggles of sin. I understand the demonic strongholds. BUT, I also understand the power of God to demolish every stronghold!

"The weapons we fight with are not the weapons of the world. On the contrary, they have divine power to demolish strongholds. We demolish arguments and every pretension that sets itself up against the knowledge of God, and we take captive every thought to make it obedient to Christ. And we will be ready to punish every act of disobedience, once your obedience is complete."
*II Corinthians 10:4-6*

I understand warfare - and that God always win! I understand that we, the believers, are victors and not victims. I understand that Satan is a liar, deceiver, illusionist and more; and that He will do anything to deceive God's people. (Remember Adam and Eve.) That is why I fight the good fight of faith. It is not faith in myself, nor faith in faith - but faith in God! I believe every word of God. There is no room in my heart for analyzing or intellectualizing the Word of God. I believe in God. PERIOD. If He says it - that's it! He says that we can live holy; in fact He commands us to be holy. He will never command us to do something that He will not equip us to do. He is Faithful! He is loving. He is so very understanding. He is Awesome. And His Word is true. AMEN!

I also understand that the Church, the building, the edifice - is open to everyone. I understand that everyone that attends the local church is not a believer- YET. I understand that we, as believers, must love unconditionally - even as Christ loves us. That withstanding - I really want to understand and help our brothers and sisters with their inner struggles. I want my brothers and sisters to understand and help me with my inner struggles. As believers - we are one! WE ARE THE BODY OF CHRIST AND WE NEED EACH OTHER! I want to share what the power of God has done for me. I want you to share what the power of God has done for you. I want us to have a mutual love and respect for one another. Amen? I want to be able to speak the truth in love and receive the truth, spoken to me, with love. I don't want to shoot the messenger, and I don't want to get shot! However, I do realize that it is not always easy to speak, or receive, God's truths; His truths are anti-world truths. Depending upon where we are in the Lord - someone might get hurt, and I mean literally hurt!

So, my cries to the Lord for His Church are heart wrenching cries. They are desperate for the hand and heart of God to help, to understand, to soothe, to correct and to guide the believer every day. They are also cries for the Body of Christ to become one!

**Jesus said:**

**"I do not pray for these alone, but also for those who will believe in Me through their word; that they all may be one, as You, Father, are in Me, and I in You; that they also may be one in Us, that the world may believe that You sent Me."**
*John 17:20-21*

These words are part of the prayers that Jesus Christ prayed for all believers! Beloved – Jesus prayed for us long before we ever came into existence! We were on His heart even then; and we still are! THANK YOU JESUS!

As Jesus prayed for us, we should in turn pray for one another; even for the generations that are to come after us. The consolation of my heart is – JESUS' PRAYERS ARE ALWAYS ANSWERED! I pray that the Church of Jesus Christ will never lose sight of this. Prayerlessness is sin!

**"Moreover, as for me, far be it from me that I should sin against the Lord in ceasing to pray for you."**
*I Samuel 12:23a*

# CHAPTER SEVEN

⋮

"Where has your lover gone, most beautiful women? Which
way did your lover turn, that we may look for him with you?
Song of Songs 6:1

So - to the crux! Again - as I promised.

## SO - YOU THINK YOU ARE READY?

When a young lady hears the words - Girl, that boy ain't
ready! What is she really hearing? What isn't he ready
for? I'm sure that you have an inexhaustive list - but allow me
to share mine.

I have personally verbalized these words to several young
ladies that I have encountered; ladies in and out of the Church.
My passion is Women's Ministry. My heart bleeds and cries for
women - females of every age group, but especially the teens and
the twenty-something's. This is such an exciting time of their
lives - yet a confusing time. As teenagers, they are struggling
with their hormones, body images and peer pressures. As twenty
something's they are struggling with becoming adults, careers,
leaving home and identity crises - Who am I? Lastly, but not
leastly, the former and the latter - their primary struggles are
with boys, men and just males. AND I CRY OUT TO MY LORD!

There is such a casualness and an expectancy of "first loves"
in these groups of young women and girls. Society pressures

these precious youths to "go out", "go with"- or just have a boy-friend (and vice versa). It's the thing to do! Sadly, the Church is extremely laxed in this area as well. Many believers (parents, guardians, ADULTS) smirk and grin at the hint of young love unfolding before their very eyes. Some are somewhat reminiscent of the perceived innocence of "dating". Yet, secretly they are fearful of its ramifications.

## QUESTION: WHERE IS DATING CONDONED IN THE BIBLE? I'M JUST ASKING!

The United States Census Bureau reported that in 2008, there were a reported 3,960,000 births. Of these births - per 1,000 women surveyed – 35.6% were women aged 15-19 years old; 85.1% were women aged 20-24 years old. The Centers For Disease Control and Prevention reported, that in 2006, there were reported 1,641,948 births. The birth rate for unmarried women was: 50.6 births per 1,000 unmarried women aged 15-44 years old; the percentage of all births to unmarried women was: 38.5%. From these noted agencies – there is a difference of over 2,000,000 births reported for unmarried women.

WHAT SHALL I CRY? What percentage of these unmarried women are born-again Christians? I'll let you look that up; the stats are alarming!

When I say born-again Christians, I mean that these are individuals who have "confessed with their mouths the Lord Jesus Christ and have believed in their hearts that God has raised Him from the dead." *(see Romans 10:9-10)* These individuals have a personal relationship with the Lord; a truly biblical salvation through Jesus Christ! Most of these young ladies are eager to be involved in a so-called "committed" relationships. BUT WHERE'S THE COMMITMENT? They are enamored with these young men and have fallen into a "trance". The young men are envisioned, by these young ladies, as their own "Prince Charming". They are ready to ride off into the sunset. Later on - they realize - that he was no prince. (I'm sure the same can be reversed - she was no princess.) But these individuals have learned some hard knock lessons of life; and now they must pay some hard prices.

The saying, "everything that glitters ain't gold", is true. There is lots of "fools" gold in the earth. Remember the song - "Everybody plays the fool sometimes; no exceptions to the rules". YEAH! Many precious youths "prefer" to learn the hard way - by experience. I call learning by this experience the hard way because none of us should have to drown before we learn to swim. (O.K. that's crazy - but you get it!) We should not have to go to jail to experience a loss of liberty. By the same token - we should not have to go to hell to experience a loss of eternal life with Jesus Christ. It isn't necessary! God has made the way. Jesus is the ONLY way, truth and life.

Jesus said to him, "I am the way, the truth, and the life. No one comes to the Father except through Me."
*John 14:6*

BELIEVE IT!

We are told that experience is the best teacher. I take exception to this statement. THE HOLY SPIRIT IS THE BEST TEACHER! He will lead and guide you into all truth. If only we would listen and obey Him we would not have to continue to practice sin and we would not have to experience a continuation of falls and regrets.

"To him who is able to keep you from falling and to present you before his glorious presence without fault and with great joy."
*Jude 24*

So, when I say to a young lady, especially one that is pursuing a relationship with one of my sons , "He ain't ready"- I mean exactly what I say! He is NOT ready for ANY relationship, other than a brother and sister relationship in the Lord. He is NOT ready to genuinely respect you, love you unconditionally, marry you and take care of you. I know there any many others who are not ready, as well! If you are <u>watching</u> over someone's soul – GOD will, by His Holy Spirit, let you know!

My sons have accepted Jesus Christ as their Savior; now they must allow Him to become their Lord. Jesus Christ must rule in their hearts and minds. There must be evidence, manifestations, lifestyle changes, mind changes, etc. At that time, they were baby Christians; they had to learn how to walk!

Looking back at the earlier mention of some mothers - those who think that their young men are either too good for some of the young ladies, or those that are mama's boys - I can state what I have learned. I have learned that - my sons truly have the capacity to be great men of God. They have been nurtured in the Word of God; they have witnessed the transforming power of God in many lives, including mine, their immediate family and many in the Church of Jesus Christ; they have made decisions to follow Christ; they were not pressured by me or the Church; they were given the Word of God on a daily basis; The Word of God was used as a home "manual"; they were corrected/disciplined; they were encouraged and they were (and are) greatly loved. HOWEVER - they have a mind of their own. If their minds (or anyone else's) are not controlled by the Spirit of Christ; if Christ is not the center of their being; if Christ is not foremost in their thinking, living and being; if Christ is not allowed to minister to them; if they are not abiding in the Vine - THEY WILL NOT BEAR ANY FRUIT! These truths hold true for all of us! Amen?

Bearing fruit is a process; it takes time. The seed (Word of God) must fall into the ground and die. Jesus' death, burial and resurrection is the greatest analogy of our spiritual growth. We must die to self. We must not allow self to raise its ugly head and thereby gain control. We must bury ourselves in Christ. We must let the old self die - let it go! Then come alive in Christ Jesus; be regenerated by the Holy Spirit.

"Therefore, if anyone is in Christ, he is a new creation; the old has gone, the new has come!"
*II Corinthians 5:17*

Somehow we have allowed the old self to come back to life. We failed to take God at His Word. We didn't believe that we could really be dead to sin and alive to Christ!

"How can a young man keep his way pure? By living according to your word. I seek you with all my heart; do not let me stray from your commands."
*Psalm 119:9-10*

## HEART TO HEART

The heart is the center of our being. We must learn to guard our hearts. A heart left unguarded is open to the onslaughts and attacks of the enemy. The breastplate of righteousness should be worn at all times; and so should all the armor.
*(see Ephesians 6:10-18)*

The heart is also the center of our personality. When we are troubled in heart (spirit) we become discouraged, fretful, sorrowful, etc. On the other hand – when we are glad in heart (spirit) we become happy, joyful, excited, etc. One can only "act" out what is in one's heart. The very words that we speak are the manifestations of the heart.

"For out of the abundance of the heart the mouth speaks."
*Matthew 12:34b*

"For out of the heart come evil thoughts, murder, adultery, sexual immorality, theft, false testimony, slander."
*Matthew 15:19*

As a person thinks in his heart, so is he. Thoughts get into the heart through the eyes, ears, and other senses. What we take into our minds (dwell on) is allowed to settle into our hearts and then the actions come forth. Beloved, we must be very careful not to confuse the spiritual heart with the natural heart. It is by the spiritual heart of a man/woman that we are defiled. We must consistently "put" the Word of God into our hearts to help us live self-controlled, moral and spiritual lives.

"Your Word I have hidden in my heart, that I might not sin against You."
*Psalm 119:11*

"I will not set nothing wicked before my eyes."
*Psalm 101:3*

Beloved, will you stand with the Psalmist and declare these words from your heart? Will you purpose in your heart today to do all that is necessary to guard your heart from the daily onslaughts of the world, the flesh and the devil? Will you "bring every thought captive to the obedience of Christ?" Please ask the Lord to "enlighten" your darkness and to reveal His precious "Light" to your heart and mind.

"For You will light my lamp; The Lord my God will enlighten my darkness."
*Psalm 18:28*

As believers, we are in right standing with God. The sinless Savior has taken our sins that we might have God's righteousness.

"God made him who had no sin to be sin for us, so that in him we might become the righteousness of God."
*II Corinthians 5:21*

We must now rise up to newness of life. Resurrection brings renewal. (Like a baptism - we are cleansed.) The natural water doesn't save us; but the Living water does!

"Having been buried with him in baptism and raised with him through your faith in the power of God, who raised him from the dead. When you were dead in your sins and in the uncircumcision of your sinful nature, God made you alive with Christ. He

forgave us all our sins, having canceled the written code, with its regulations, that was against us and that stood opposed to us; he took it away, nailing it to the cross."
*Colossians 2:12-14*

Oh what a cleansing! Our wills must be given over to God. "Not my will, but thy will be done." Jesus said that! QUESTION: DID WE FORGET?

In my conversations with many girls, teens, young women, etc. I am very quick to "warn" them of this impending process that is taking place in their lives; growing up! God designed all humans and He knows the complexities of our lives. The transformation from girl to woman is amazing, and challenging. God sees this transformation as pure and holy; so should we. It has always been my heartfelt prayer and cry to the Lord - that my sons would never disrespect, defraud or misuse any female. I have taught my sons godly values and given them godly principles to abide by. Most importantly, I have, by the grace of God, exemplified godly behavior in our home, as well as in the Church and the community. I have been very transparent with my sons. I have informed them of some of my past sins and God's forgiveness. But most importantly, God, by His Holy Spirit, has given us, and shown to us, the greatest example in life: His Son - Jesus Christ! (You can't get any better than that!)

My prayer was that they would learn from these godly teachings; apply godly wisdom to their own lives; always exemplify godly behavior; have a heart knowledge of God and not just a head knowledge; live self-controlled holy lives in an unholy world; allow Christ to be the center of their lives; allow His Spirit to transform their lives and always treat young ladies as sisters in Christ. (Like the Apostle Paul speaking to Timothy and Titus.) I would also pray the same prayer for the young ladies. (Maybe that was too much - you think?)

Several young ladies, that befriended my sons, did not have a personal relationship with Christ. In fact, several were from households predominantly maintained by women; households with more than one father and households that did not know

71

Jesus Christ as their Savior. (What an excellent opportunity to show the love of Christ!) I was very glad to know that my sons were witnessing - but I was extremely watchful of the enemy. I know that devil! And I know young people as well. As I previously stated, my sons were taught to respect and treat young ladies very special. They did so; they made them feel real special!

What I know from experience is this - when a young man makes a young lady feel "special" - she, in turn, wants to make him "feel" special as well. Her "natural" response is sex. I continuously cautioned my sons about special attractions, i.e. "What makes this young lady different from the rest?" I warned them about "ministering" one on one to the opposite sex. Being young Christians they were warned that babies could not minister to babies!

Some of the young ladies did accept Jesus Christ as their Savior. PRAISE GOD! Then there were some, through naivety or collusion that would allow my sons to enter their homes for Bible Study. YEAH RIGHT! I would counsel both of them and warn them of this perceived innocence. (CAN'T YOU SEE THE DEVIL IN THIS?) But my sons were determined to show me that they were growing up; both physically and spiritually. I knew that they were baby Christians, and so were the young ladies. I would use the analogy of natural babies in the cribs to drive my point. It takes a mother and father to assist, to train, to nourish and to nurture babies. It also takes a mother and father (in the Lord) to assist, train, nourish and nurture spiritual babies. I counseled them to stay connected to their father and me, to seek godly counsel/mentors - AND DON'T GO BACK TO THAT GIRL'S HOME ALONE!

I have personally witnessed parents who would allow boys to enter their daughter's bedroom - TO STUDY! What's wrong with the family room? Beloved - that's a step in the wrong direction. This enemy is a liar! He pulls you in like a magnet. Believe me -opposites do attract! It is a natural, human and God-ordained design for God's creations. BLESS GOD!

Now my sons may not have been ready for genuine commitments or marriage, but as young, virile men - they were, and are, ready for sex. YES - SEX! Like it or not the Church's youths are ready, willing and able to have sex - and lots of it! A great majority of our youths are not ashamed or disgraced by having unmarried sex. By the age of twenty many of these youths will have had sex with multiple partners. Our culture is inundated with "casual sex" - more aptly labeled today as "sex with benefits" or "sex with favors". No marriage commitments - JUST ANIMALISTIC BEHAVIOR!

"Treat younger men as brothers, older women as mothers, <u>and younger women as sisters, with absolute purity.</u>"
*I Timothy 5:1b-2*

Girl - that boy ain't ready! And neither are you!
QUESTION: WHAT DOES THE WORD OF GOD SAY?

Oftentimes when mature believers minister to carnal believers (and even unbelievers) there tends to be a resistance of some kind. What I mean is - the question frequently arises-
"Did you forget when you use to _____?"
I have been told by believers and unbelievers, "You know what you did!" However, I don't remember reading in the Bible – "You shall only speak to others about the things you didn't do or say. You shall not speak as if you never committed any sin. You must take into account that nobody's perfect. "Always go easy, don't_____!" (Fill in the blanks. I know that you have heard them before; maybe you have said them.) The Word of God says -

"For all have sinned and fall short of the Glory of God."
*Romans 3:23*

That includes me and the holiest person on Earth! NO EXCEPTIONS!

But the Word of God also says –

"Preach the Word; be prepared in season and out of season; correct, rebuke and encourage - with great patience and careful instruction. For the time will come when men will not put up with sound doctrine. Instead, to suit their own desires, they will gather around them a great number of teachers to say what their itching ears want to hear. They will turn their ears away from the truth and turn aside to myths. But you, keep your head in all situations, endure hardship, do the work of an evangelist, discharge all the duties of your ministry."
*II Timothy 4:2-5*

In essence, the Apostle Paul was telling "young" Timothy - to always be ready, whether the time was opportune for preaching the gospel or not. By opportune - he was indicating that there would be times when Timothy would have to just say what God told him to say - regardless of the situation. SPEAK THE WORD MAN/WOMAN OF GOD!
Whether we are speaking the truth of God's Word to believers or unbelievers we must know that the Bible is clear that God's accepted time is today.

"Today, if you will hear His voice, do not harden you hearts."
*Hebrews 4:7*

"Behold, now is the accepted time; behold now is the day of salvation."
*II Corinthians 6:2b*

We are to witness any time, all the time, in any place and in all places. (of course being led by the Holy Spirit) The Apostle Paul is a great example to us. He witnessed everywhere; in a prison, in the midst of being stoned, on a sinking ship and in the final days of his life.
Of course everyone will not want to hear it —BUT —

"How then, can they call on the one they have not believed in? And how can they believe on the one in whom they have not heard? And how can they hear without someone preaching to them? And how can they preach unless they are sent?"
*Romans 10:14-15a*

As believers of Jesus Christ we have been sent!

"Go therefore and make disciples of all the nations, baptizing them in the name of the Father and of the Son and of the Holy Spirit, teaching them to observe all things that I have commanded you; and lo, I am with you always, even to the end of the age." Amen.
*Matthew 28:18-19*

These are the final words of Jesus while on earth. Sharing God's Word is vital! Believers are to share God's Word, without mixing it with opinions or the world's philosophies! God chose us, His followers, to tell people about Him. He could have chosen angels, but He didn't. Our love for God should be ample reason to tell everyone about Him. It also shows our obedience to our Father. A disobedient Christian is an oxymoron! Don't you think so?

Beloved - we are in terrible times! When I read the Word of God - it is as if I am reading today's news. The Book of Timothy is an excellent study - READ IT! So, my carnal friends - who do I obey? I'm sure you already know the answer. Albeit - it is not always easy to speak the truth in love; but it is always necessary!

"You shall know the Truth, and the Truth will make you free."
*John 8:32*

When you know and apply the Truth; the Truth will make you free. I am not rewriting the scripture; I am just re-emphasizing the need to use wisdom. Wisdom is the application of knowledge!

BELOVED – BE FREE TODAY!

# CHAPTER EIGHT

⋮

"Brothers, I do not consider myself yet to have taken hold of
it. But one thing I do: Forgetting what is behind and straining
toward what is ahead. I press on toward what is ahead.
I press on toward the goal to win the prize for which
God has called me heavenward in Christ Jesus."
Philippians 3:13-14

**GOING FORWARD —**

For me, and for so many others, the clock did not stop when
I learned that my sons were sexually promiscuous. (You do
know that the DNA is powerful!) An assessment of my family's
"tree" revealed a lineage of sexual immorality (including out of
wedlock children). HOWEVER - the Word of God says - the
Blood of Jesus cleanses us from ALL unrighteousness. It further
states that Jesus Christ IS the same yesterday (in the days of His
life on earth), today (as our High Priest in heaven), and forevermore (to secure and consummate our salvation). (*see Hebrews
13:8*) I also take these words personally. The POWER of Jesus
Christ is the same yesterday (*my forefathers*), today (*me and my
children*) and forevermore (*my grandchildren, great-grandchil-
dren, etc.*).

Since Jesus Christ came to reconcile fallen man back to God -
then ALL our sins are forgiven. The Blood of Jesus HAS cleansed
us of every sin. There is NO sin, family or generational curse,

soul ties, blood line, hex, witchcraft, etc. that is more powerful than the blood of Jesus! "For it reaches to the highest mountain and it flows to the lowest valley. It's the Blood that gives me strength from day to day. It will NEVER lose its power!"

The Blood of Jesus can never be diluted or weaken due to cultures, generations, times, seasons, blood lines, people, places or things! It is the essence of our forgiveness and cleansing; it is the Atonement. So, if we know Jesus Christ as our Savior all our sins are covered with the Blood of Jesus Christ; including my saved sons (and your children as well – if they are saved). PRAISE GOD!

The problem is that MOST of us do not know how or have not appropriated the Blood of Jesus to our everyday lives, so we remain deceived. This is turn allows us to continue to PRACTICE SIN! (making sin a habit)

"Christ redeemed us from the curse of the law by becoming a curse for us, for it is written; "Cursed is everyone who is hung on a tree."
*Galatians 3:13*

The believer IS delivered from the curse (that the law brings) through Jesus Christ, who became a curse for us. *(see Galatians – Chapter 3)*

Every jot and tittle of God's Word can be trusted!

"Heaven and earth will pass away, but My words will by no means pass away".
*Matthew 24:35*

## WHAT GOD WANTED TO SHOW ME!

Oftentimes when a parent is confronted with their children's sin feelings of shame, embarrassment, disgrace and downright madness emerges! Questions often arise - How could you do this to ME? What will people say about ME? How am I supposed to face the Church? What did I do to deserve this? And let's not forget my favorite - Didn't I tell you that this was going to happen?

Various emotions come into play; and play with my mind they did! Night and day the enemy would taunt me with the words - How can YOU face those Church folks? How can YOU tell anybody about your family's situation? How will someone continue to follow YOU? YOU might as well step down from leadership! YOU ought to be ashamed of yourself! YOUR children are a disgrace! How can YOU still love and admire YOUR children? Look at ALL they have done to YOU! Look at how they have messed up those young ladies lives! All the taunting and emotions were screaming at me to run, run, *run Forrest run*! I just wanted to go into hiding - ANYWHERE! I felt so overwhelmed with guilt, disgrace, shame and embarrassment for me, my children, the young ladies, the Church and everybody with eyes! And yes - it all became personal; my children did this to ME! Then there was that moment when I would say to God, "Here - take them they are yours! I did my best!" I -I - I - I - I - I - I - I! God simply responded, 'So NOW you want to give them to me?'

Dear friend - isn't it ironic that when the children are exceeding or progressing very well in academics, sports, good behavior, good manners, social graces, going to Church regularly, participating in Church, being well-spoken of, graduating top of the class, landing a great job, having notoriety, etc. - they are OUR children? We take a spiritual "strut"; sit back and lean on our "look what I did" graces and loudly applaud the work of OUR hands. YET - the moment the cookie begins to crumble or the bottom begins to fall out we run for cover screaming for God to do something. Please Lord do something -anything; do it NOW; make it go away!

Personally, when I learned of my sons' discretions (they came rather repetitiously) I wanted to run back to my old world of fantasies. I knew that in that world, my world, I could make it all go away. I simply would substitute the bad for the good. My situation would instantly turn into something good, or someone else's mess. My confusion, chaos and pain would be someone else's. I, in turn, would be there to help comfort, soothe, counsel, etc. It was perfectly alright for me to be on the outside looking in - but NEVER could anything, that I viewed so disgraceful, be really happening to me!

I have been told by a very dear friend that I live in a "bubble". Beloved - I really do believe that the people of God, Christians/ believers, can live above the standards of this world. I believe that at any conversation, at work or at play, we can interject the Name of Jesus (for the good) and engage Him in every way possible. He IS the answer to ALL our needs, concerns, problems, etc. I personally believe that some people have a problem with me being an optimist. Truly, I want God's best for everyone. Believers in Christ have His (the Father's) Best! So why not live it out to its' fullest? That's my take! What about yours?

What I did not take to heart was that my sons were hurting, as well. They were well aware of their sins. They knew the hurt, pain, shame and disappointment that they caused our family, the Church, the young ladies and their families, me, themselves and especially the Lord. Somehow – (due to my own selfishness) I missed the opportunity to allow them to share their pain with me, to cry along with me, to hold each other. I know they cried - but we didn't share our sadness. THANK GOD FOR HEALING; GOD'S LOVE AND COMPASSION COVERED ALL OF US! I did "awaken" to the fact that they needed and wanted their mama; and I was there for them. PRAISE GOD!

QUESTIONS: DOES ANYONE FEEL ME? HAVE YOU BEEN THERE MY FRIEND? ARE YOU THERE NOW?

I want to assure you that if you have ever been acquainted with these scenarios, you know full well the extinct of my pain. You also must know that when you "Cast your cares upon the Lord - He will sustain you." (*see Psalm 55:22*) God takes those cares and concerns and makes them His own; they now belong to Him. And so do you!

I wanted more for my children. I did not want them to "experiment" with sex, as I had. These young ladies were not a "hands on project", requiring trial and error. They were precious souls in need of a Savior and Godly love. I knew that my sons and these young ladies were anxious about having a "special" relationship and that they were getting too close to each other. I knew that neither of them were ready! Especially for babies!

I also believe that children deserve two well-adjusted, God-fearing, loving and nurturing parents. I truly believe in family, as God ordained it; marriage and children within the biblical context. I'M NOT NAIEVE! I know the world that we live in and the people, including church folks! But most importantly, I know that God can do anything. I know because I was once in my children's shoes. BUT GOD!

I did not want my children, or anyone, to "settle" for anything less than God's best for their lives. Far too many Christians today are "settling" for the enemy's crumbs instead of waiting for God's banquet!

FACING THE GIANTS -

Sometimes our problems, concerns, troubles, etc. seem insurmountable! They seem to overwhelm, burden, control and immobilize us; we can't go forward or backward - we are stuck in neutral! That's exactly the way I felt. I wanted so much to move on - to get past this - but the reality kept me immobilized. I kept looking back and the "whys" of life were like obstacles that kept tripping me; they were coming too fast and I couldn't jump over them! My strength was gone and I just laid down and cried out to God; day after day after day.

Then on one particular morning, I remember speaking to God about my family situation. He spoke so gently, yet so profoundly to my heart. He ministered to me and showed me my "real" self. As a child, and even into adulthood, I had problems facing "giants". I never liked confrontations. I always wanted to take the path of least resistance. If there was a mountain in my way - I would simply go around it. I didn't want to speak to it nor climb it. It didn't matter to me that I was taking the long way around - I would just quickly slip into my fantasy world and make it an adventure! Needless to say - there were multiple lessons that I did not learn; and "giants" that I did not conquer!

But on another day, thereafter, while devoting time to God; He spoke to me about David and Goliath. (I'm sure you know the story.) The story of David and Goliath was one of my favorite Sunday School lessons. I can still remember the students in our Sunday School class marching to the beat of - "How did David kill the Giant? He put a little rock in his sling sling sling and let it go with a zing zing zing and hit the giant on the head that's how he killed the giant." I still smile when I sing or hear that song. This childhood memory has great spiritual connotations, truths and principles for me today.

God reminded me of what David did AFTER he killed Goliath, the giant. David took the giants' sword and cut off Goliath's head! (*see I Samuel 17*) The head reminded me of the origination of my problems. Once the problems were exposed, or dealt with, the concerns died. I could not allow the enemy to get into my head. I could not think, ponder, meditate or worry about the things that I had already cast upon the Lord. David knew in his heart that the God of Israel was with him. All the other men, including King Saul, would not go out to fight Goliath. David took recollection of the lion and bear that he had already encountered, and killed! I too would have to take recollection as to what God had already done for me! I had to appropriate the Word of God, with my faith in God, and kill this giant that was wreaking havoc in my mind! You see - the mind is the devil's battlefield. Just as Goliath taunted the Israelites, the devil taunts us as well; and he was taunting me day and night. The natural mind requires a body to "carry out" its' mission. If the head is removed from the body, then the body in turn is lifeless. It can no longer carry out the enemy's mission of worry, fret, regret, anger, unforgiveness, not walking in love or running away.

"You will keep him in perfect peace, whose mind is stayed on You, because he trusts in you."
*Isaiah 26:3*

"And be renewed in the spirit of your mind."
*Ephesians 4:23*

"Therefore gird up the loins of your mind, be sober, and rest your hope fully upon the grace that is to be brought to you at the revelation of Jesus Christ."
*I Peter 1:13*

The mind is extremely powerful! If left unchecked it will "team up" with the flesh and do extreme damage to the life of the believer. But a mind that is focused on God will join forces with the Holy Spirit and walk in deliverance! Beloved – we must keep our minds stayed on Him at all times!

CAUTION: NOW DON'T CUT YOUR HEAD OFF; OR ANYONE ELSE'S! THIS FOR ME WAS SYMBOLIC; NOT LITERAL!

The Word of God was magnified in my heart and mind as I spoke with the Apostle Paul –

"I HAVE BEEN CRUCIFIED WITH CHRIST AND I NO LONGER LIVE, BUT CHRIST LIVES IN ME. THE LIFE I LIVE IN THE BODY, I LIVE BY FAITH IN THE SON OF GOD, WHO LOVED ME AND GAVE HIMSELF FOR ME."
*Galatians 2:20*

Yes, I screamed, I am crucified; I am dead! I realized that I could no longer resurrect those things that were now buried; cast into the sea of forgetfulness - NEVER - to be remembered anymore. FREEDOM! Free to go on in spite of the what, where, why or when's! Free to face the giants - and to SEE them fall! And yes beloved - they did fall. They did not fall in the way(s) in which I thought or wanted them to, but by the way God designed them to. Actually, the first "giant" I came to understand - was me! The enemy was actually me! The adage, "It is what it is", became a truth to my heart and spirit. I had not allowed these realities to become truths for fear of having to deal with them. But, there I was - now - facing the giants and seeing the "real" me at the same time. I thank and praise God for "enlightening" me with His Truth!

"For You will light my lamp; the Lord my God will enlighten my darkness. For by You I can run against a troop and by My God I can leap over a wall."
*Psalm 18:28-29*

PRAISE GOD!

What about you beloved? Where are you in the "valley" of truths and decisions? Who or what are your "giants"? Have you allowed the Holy Spirit to "free" you of the giants in your life? I told you before - this little book, with all its twists and turns, is a message from God to "free" us. GET FREE MY BROTHERS AND SISTERS - AND STAY FREE!

"But the free gift is not like the offense. For if by one man's offense many died, much more grace of God and the gift by the grace of the one Man, Jesus Christ, abounded to many. And the gift is not like that which came through the one who sinned. For the judgment which came from one offense resulted in condemnation, but the free gift which came from many offenses resulted in justification."
*Romans 5:15-16 (New King James Version)*

# CHAPTER 9

**"Walk in the Spirit and you will not fulfill the lust of the flesh."**
**Galatians 5:16 (KJV)**

**GOING ON – –**

I n spite of all the roadblocks and setbacks in our lives we must keep walking! To walk means- to progress by lifting and setting down each foot in turn; never having both feet off the ground at once. The NIV states to, "live by the Spirit." We should take each step of the Christian life in dependence on the Holy Spirit so that we may have victory over the flesh and all its activities.

How many times have we remarked, "I'm going through"! This statement could relate to a number of things, i.e. sickness, disease, marital distress, financial straits, emotional issues, strained relationships, family conflicts, church folks, spiritual issues, etc. I believe that all of us have said or heard someone use this expression to indicate a particular time or season in their lives. Usually it is, or was, referred to as a time or place in life that is, or was, not pleasant!

The Holy Spirit ministered to me regarding my "going through" times. The operative phrase was, and is, "going through". This indicated to me that I was going to make it out as long as I kept walking through the situation. But I had to walk (live) by faith and not by sight. (*see II Corinthians 5:7*) I had to live by faith in the reality of His presence and the promises of His Word concerning my future. The Holy Spirit's words of comfort thrilled my heart. To have God's assurance that He would always be with me; that I did not have to sink into the depths of despair and allow the enemy to beat me up; and that the "promises" of God were real - became the truths that I took to heart and lived by. God's truths, in His Word, was my meditation! I knew that in the "process" of being made over by God, and that in this "fiery" trial of life - I would come forth as pure gold. OH- BUT THE FIRE!

"Beloved, do not think it strange concerning the fiery trial which is to try you, as though some strange thing happened to you; but rejoice to the extent that you partake in Christ's sufferings, you may also be glad with exceeding joy."
*I Peter 4:12-13*

As believers we want to "come out" as pure gold, but do not want to "go through" the fire. Beloved - that is an impossible task. God must purify His gold IN the fire. I don't know of any fire that does not burn! There is a purifying process, a cleansing process and a removal of dross process BEFORE the gold comes out. The dilemma of our coming out or going through is that we do not know exactly WHEN it will happen. If we allow our minds to focus on a particular time, a time that we believe the encounter should be over, then we will be sorely displeased. The Word of God says in *Ecclesiastes 3:1*, "There is a time and a season for every activity under the heaven." It goes on to state those particular times and seasons. (*Read Ecclesiastes - Chapter 3*) Nowhere does it state the "chronos" times. We cannot put a clock or calendar to these times. We must walk by faith; our Christian walk IS a faith walk!

KNOWING OUR SEASONS

It is equally important and imperative that we know our seasons. Oftentimes we have said, or have heard someone say, must boastfully, "It's my season!" The usual, or common, understanding is that this person is speaking about the time of life that he/she is encountering at this specific time; they are speaking of where they are now, and it is usually a pleasant time of life. BUT - I must interject my beloved to ask you - or whomever is making the statement - what exactly is it your season of, or for? Do you really know what season you are in? Beloved, knowing your season will help in the process of walking through it! Is it your season of prosperity? Is it your season of quietness? Is it your season of breakthroughs? Is it your season of suffering? Suffering? YES! (Please read the Book of Peter and the Book of Acts.)

In our seasons - God is preparing us for our harvest. In the natural - the "seed" is planted to produce a harvest; yet all "seeds" cannot be planted at the same time. There is a particular "season" in which the particular seed must be planted to produce the particular harvest. For example, you don't plant tomato seeds in the winter, do you? With the natural seed, we must assess the soil. Is there any crabgrass, grubs or something eating up the seed? (I could really go on with this- but I won't!) Yes - it's preparation and that of itself is a process! (You know it is!)

Also, there is a digging process, a cultivation process, a planting process and a waiting process BEFORE the harvest comes. PROCESS - PROCESS - PROCESS! This word sounds so simple; yet so unnerving. Most of us, believers, will not wait! I want it now! Yesterday is too late! (That's not you of course.)

But honestly, do you really know what season you are in - now?

"Like snow in summer or rain in harvest."
*Proverbs 26:1a*

Sometimes our seasons are inundated with CHANGE! But as the Word of God declares - it can and will – "snow" in your season of summer. When your life seems to be in full bloom, when things are going great, when you have the peace of God and you are at peace with God and others - your season can do a drastic change, without notice! What do you do? You must ADJUST! Adjust is defined as - arrange, put in the correct order or position; make suitable; harmonize; make oneself suited to. Oh — it's still the summer season, but with an adjustment; with a twist. The adjustment does not have to be resultant of anything that you have done; it could very well be God! How will you handle this noted distraction in your life? How will you handle this interrupting change? Will you learn to adjust?

Well - we must first go to the Creator of the Universe. We must go to the Lord God, our Father, through His Son Jesus, by the power of the Holy Spirit and inquire of Him. CRY OUT TO HIM! He knows exactly what is going on. He is El Roi; the God who sees. He is Omniscient; He knows. We must go before Him with worship and praise. We must go to Him with thanksgiving and ascribe greatness to His Name. Yes - we must acknowledge Him and show Him great worship. He is still worthy to be praised - no matter what the situation, problem or circumstance might be. It is something about talking to the Father that puts things in its proper perspective. "Our ways are not His ways; neither are our thoughts His thoughts."

When we receive the mind of Christ, on every matter, "old things are passed away and behold all things become new." (salvation) We have a new spin on all old adages. God shows up and makes it all clear. Whether we want to believe it or not - God is always right! We have to trust Him in all of our seasons of life. Eventually - "this too shall pass". And even if it doesn't - our hearts and minds will be transformed to the image of Christ. We will learn to accept by faith God's plans for our lives. Amen? What a change! What an adjustment! We all need them in our lives; they help to mold our character and shape our integrity. Then we go on -on to the next season in our lives. And there will be more!

"Trust in the Lord with all your heart, and lean not on your own understanding; In all your ways acknowledge Him, And He shall direct your paths."
*Proverbs 3:5-6*

Beloved, that is something that I learned during <u>one</u> of my "going through" seasons. I had to adjust my present attitude, and not my circumstances. I had to face the fact that there would not only be additions to our family but to the young ladies families as well. I had to accept that even though this was not what I wanted, it was happening - and yes to me! I wanted God to change things for me. BUT - He wanted me to change my mindset (a mental attitude that can influence one's interpretation of events or situations). I had to learn how to adjust and keep on walking! And I did! PRAISE GOD!

Consider this beloved: While in our seasons of life - God is preparing us for our harvest. But we must be in position to listen (to the voice of God); learn (the essential lessons of life usually by "seasoned" people of God, or "seed sowers") and be led (by the Holy Spirit). Listening means that we must be silent (SHH!). In order to learn we must have teachable spirits. (You don't know it all!) To be led by the Holy Spirit we must submit, yield and place ourselves under the total control of God's Spirit. (HE will lead and guide us into all truth.) This is a necessary process. It's called preparation (something done to make ready; be disposed or willing to).

## CHURCH OF JESUS CHRIST - ARE YOU READY?

Because I birthed, reared and loved my sons - I knew them. I knew their habits, ideas, idiosyncrasies, nuances, likes, dislikes, fears, etc. In actuality, I knew them better than they knew themselves. (Sound familiar?) I knew them because I studied them; I prayed for them; I spent time with them; I nurtured them; I mentored them; I encouraged them; I disciplined them and I loved them - and still do! Our hearts were meshed together and threaded by the cord of the Word of God and agape love. So - I might ask - does it stand to reason that I had a personal relationship with them, and that I desired God's best for them? Yes I did, and still do!

## QUESTION: IS THE CHURCH OF JESUS CHRIST DOING THE SAME FOR PEOPLE TODAY?

Beloved – let us answer these questions from the heart. Are we, the Church of Jesus Christ, nurturing people or only noticing all their flaws? Are we disciplining people when we should be discipling them, and vice versa? Are we accusing people when we should be admonishing them? Are we excusing people when we should be exhorting them? Are we warning people or growing weary of them? (I TOLD THEM ONCE AND I AM NOT GOING TO TELL THEM AGAIN!) Are we pointing our fingers at people when we should be pointing them to God? Are we praying for people and with people or <u>preying</u> on them? Are we living exemplary lives in front of people or excusing our non-Christian behavior to them? (EVERYBODY GOT SOMETHING! NO BODY IS PERFECT! I'M ONLY HUMAN! GOD KNOWS MY HEART!)

Have we, the Church of Jesus Christ, become students of our fellow man or have we made them statues carved out by neglect, greed, unforgiveness, etc. - that have only a form of godliness? Where's the power of God? Are we Christ's witnesses or the world's waitresses? What are we serving people? Are we truly servants? Does anyone see Christ in us or has the light gone out? And Church - if we are the light - then why is the world so dark?

Oh Beloved – What is <u>our</u> present State of the Union? The Body of Christ is in sin and turmoil! There is just too much mess in the Church of Jesus Christ! (Don't look at the building - look at the Body!) Two consolations (one is not really a consolation at all) is that; this apathy is not directed towards one particular local church or denomination. It is inclusive of the Body of Christ, the Church - THE CALLED OUT ONES! The other is that; "the gates of hell shall not prevail against the Church of Jesus Christ." Hallelujah!

## QUESTION: CHURCH - ARE WE REALLY READY TO CHANGE?

Beloved - God has given us HIS remedy for our pain, shame and disgrace. It seems to be extremely difficult for saints, believers, Christians to call themselves wicked; even though God says that we are (or can be)! It is equally difficult for saints, believers, Christians to humble themselves; even though God commands us to.

"If my people, who are called by my name, will humble themselves and pray and seek my face and turn from their wicked ways, then will I hear from heaven and will forgive their sin and will heal their land."
*II Chronicles 7:14*

## LET'S EXPOUND ON THIS SCRIPTURE.

HUMBLE: marked by meekness or modesty; unpretentious; lowly.

"You save the humble, but your eyes are on the haughty to bring them low."
*II Samuel 22:28*

There is a total disregard for humility in the Church of Jesus Christ. Many believers perceive meekness (humility) to be a sign of weakness. However, meekness (humility) is strength under control!
We are instructed in the Word of God to "humble ourselves under the mighty hand of God and He will exalt us in due time."

## CHURCH - ARE WE READY TO OBEY GOD?

**PRAY: supplicate, beseech, appeal, petition, entreat.**

Then I said, "O LORD, God of heaven, the great and awesome God, who keeps his covenant of love with those who love him and obey his commands, let your ear be attentive and your eyes open to hear the prayer your servant is praying before you day and night for your servants, the people of Israel. I confess the sins we Israelites, including myself and my father's house, have committed against you. We have acted very wickedly toward you. We have not obeyed the commands, decrees and laws you gave your servant Moses."
*Nehemiah 1:5-7*

Prayer is work and most Christians are lazy! God is not being consulted in most of our requests; our ways are not committed to Him. When our motives for praying are genuine and sincere, God hears and answers!

Jesus said, "Ask and it shall be given." So – if we are not receiving answers to our prayers we must check ourselves!

## CHURCH - ARE WE READY TO OBEY GOD?

**SEEK: to search for; to try to reach.**

"They entered into a covenant to seek the Lord, the God of their fathers, with all their heart and soul."
*II Chronicles 15:12*

As believers in Jesus Christ, and His followers, we too have entered a covenant (binding agreement) with Him. The primary problem with many Christians is that we feel that we can easily cancel the agreement whenever we choose. NOT SO!

"We are not our own, we have been bought with a price." The precious blood of Jesus should cause every Christian to give themselves whole-heartedly and sacrificially to seeking the Lord and doing ALL that He requires!

## CHURCH - ARE WE READY TO OBEY GOD?

TURN: reverse, become, rotate, avert (to prevent or keep from happening).

"Turn from evil and do good; seek peace and pursue it."
*Psalm 34:14*

To understand that we must turn – we must first understand that we are going in the wrong direction! For many Christians there is either; a "lack of understanding"; a rebellious spirit; or a downright refusal to obey God's Word!

Now, we are instructed to "go after" peace. What are you waiting for?

Jesus said that the "Holy Spirit would lead and guide us into all Truth."

## CHURCH - ARE WE READY TO OBEY GOD?

## FROM OUR (THAT'S YOU AND ME!)

WICKED: immoral, bad, evil, ungodly, unsound, sinful.

"The Lord detests the way of the wicked but He loves those who pursue righteousness."
*Proverbs 15:9*

There it is – God says that we (believers, Christians) have wicked ways! He means that our ways, beliefs, thinking, actions, lifestyles, etc. are NOT in agreement with His. God is always right! Let us now agree with Him.

Jesus has "become for us wisdom from God – that is, our righteousness, holiness and redemption." Now, follow Him!

## CHURCH - ARE WE READY TO OBEY GOD?

**BELOVED** - these are God's commands to us - His Children! These are not options!

Yet, as believers in Christ, we tend to think so. There are ALWAYS conditions for God's promises. BUT HE IS FAITHFUL!

"If we are faithless, He will remain faithful, for He cannot disown Himself."
*II Timothy 2:13*

**THEN:** at that time; subsequently or soon afterward (*when we obey Him/when we do our part*).

"Then will I hear from heaven and will forgive their sin and will heal their land."

"This is the confidence we have in approaching God; that if we ask anything according to His will, HE HEARS US. And if we know that He hears us - whatever we ask- we know that we have what we asked of Him."
*I John 5:14-15*

## WHAT'S GOING ON?

So - what exactly is our problem? Is it sin, self, Satan or just our good old pride? The Bible is God's Word; God is speaking. Are we listening? This Book will keep us away from sin - or sin will keep us away from this Book. There is always a choice! To serve sin, self or Satan is a choice! Who or what have you chosen my friend? Who or what do you serve? God, by His providential love and understanding of weak, emaciated flesh, serves as our Teacher. Every teacher gives tests! (Right?) God gives His students (that's us) open book tests! PRAISE GOD! The answers to all of our tests (in life) are found in God's Book; the Bible. OPEN THE BOOK! GET TO KNOW THE TEACHER! BE THE TEACHER'S PET! Go ahead - get your passing grade and move to the next level! Sadly - some of us like failing! (We call it repeating the grade.) Listen - spiritual retardation is prevalent in the Church of Jesus Christ. Mind you - we would not desire retardation in the natural sense.

(God bless those of you who are experiencing this; He gives you grace to endure!) Yet we allow, compromise and make allowances, (AKA excuses) for retardation in the spiritual sense. GO FIGURE!

## SO - I REPEAT THE QUESTION TO THE CHURCH: ARE WE READY TO CHANGE!

YES!!!! (I HEAR YOU OUT THERE!) Beloved - there can be no other answer. It will take total obedience to the Word of God. If we don't adhere purposefully, totally and wholeheartedly to the Word of God - what will happen to us? What will happen to our children? What will happen to those who have not come into God's Kingdom?

"Son of man, I have made you a watchman for the house of Israel; so hear the word I speak and give them warning from me. When I say to a wicked man, 'You will surely die,' and you do not warn him or speak out to dissuade him from his evil ways in order to save his life, that wicked man will die for his sin, and I will hold you accountable for his blood. But if you do warn the wicked man and he does not turn from his wickedness or from his evil ways, he will die for his sin; but you will have saved yourself. Again, when a righteous man turns from his righteousness and does evil, and I put a stumbling block before him, he will die. Since you did not warn him, he will die for his sin. The righteous things he did will not be remembered and I will hold you accountable for his blood. But if you do warn the righteous man not to sin and he does not sin, he will surely live because he took warning, and you will have saved yourself."
*Ezekiel 3:17-21*

The Prophet Ezekiel was responsible for warning these people, but each person was personally responsible for his/her response to the warning! When Pontius Pilate wanted to release Jesus Christ - because he could not find anything worthy of his death - the naïve Jews cried out to him to, "Let His (Jesus') blood be on us and our children."
(*see Matthew 27:24-25*) Now look at the nation of Israel! Now look at us today!

Beloved - let's not give a hint of The Body of Christ <u>attempting</u> to re-crucify our Lord and Savior Jesus Christ by our willful acts of disobedience and immoral lifestyles. Let's not inwardly make this same fatal declaration by our outward expressions of intense selfishness, ungodliness, and our willingness to accept the "spirit" of the world. Amen?

**AND LET US THANK GOD FOR JESUS! HIS BLOOD CLEANSES US FROM ALL UNRIGHTEOUSNESS!**

# CHAPTER 10

### ⋮

**"But they that wait on the Lord.."**
**Isaiah 40:31a**

## WHAT WAS GOD IMPRESSING ON MY HEART AND TO THE CHURCH?

As I continued to speak to God and wait for His direction in this writing, I could hear the words, "Girl, he ain't ready" being translated into words: WORLD - THE CHURCH AIN'T READY! I thought it to be strange but this sad commentary is our reality. Oh yes - these truths began to be penned: To the world -

The Church is ready to embrace you - but not to inform you of the wages of sin. The Church is ready to love you in an EROS kind of way - but not love you in an AGAPE way. The Church is ready to give you religion - but not demonstrate to you a Godly relationship. The Church is ready to say they have a personal relationship with Jesus Christ - but will keep the relationship with you private. (You know what I mean!) The Church is ready to entertain you - but not to enlighten you with God's Word. The Church is ready to deceive you - but not to dedicate their lives to what they say they believe. The Church is ready to deliver a message that damns you to hell - but not lead you to the deliverer. The Church is ready to take you to a church building - but not ready to take up their cross daily and follow Jesus. The Church is ready to covet you - but not to cover you with the blood of Jesus. The Church is ready to talk about you - but not talk to God for you. The Church is ready to socialize with you - but not ready to be sober minded about you. The Church is ready to play with you - but not ready to pray for you. The Church says that they are ready - but they really are not. The Church says that they are holy – but the world says that they are hypocrites! YOU SEE IT EVERYDAY - DON'T YOU?

My heart's cry was, and still is, Lord - help us; have mercy on us and come to us quickly! Church - Do we really love the Lord? Remember the Israelites? They would pray, love God, sin, repent, be reconciled to God - pray, love God, sin, repent, be reconciled to God — and on and on and on - an endless vicious cycle! (Does this look like someone you know?)

BUT GOD!! All throughout the scriptures - the love of God, the forgiveness of God, the mercies of God, the blood of Jesus and the power of the Holy Spirit reeks through its' pages. Beloved, can you see the Church and yourself in this writing? Do you find any of this to be true? What are you going to do about it? ARE YOU READY TO CRY OUT?

Revival starts with you and me! LORD REVIVE US AGAIN!

"Your vine is cut down, it is burned with fire; at your rebuke your people perish. Let your hand rest on the man at your right hand, the son of man you have raised up for yourself. Then we will not turn away from you; revive us, and we will call on your name. Restore us, O Lord God Almighty; make your face shine upon us, that we may be saved."
*Psalm 80:16-19*

## SO - HOW ABOUT IT CHURCH?

Are you ready to go to your sanctuary, bow before the King of Kings and the Lord of Lords, REPENT of your sins? Are you ready to receive forgiveness, then praise and worship God? Are you ready to submit, yield yourselves totally to His Hands and allow the Potter to make and mold you? (*see Jeremiah 18*). Are you ready to stay on the wheel and in His Will? He has a perfect plan for your life.

"For I know the plans I have for you, declares the Lord, plans to prosper you and not to harm you, plans to give you hope and a future."
*Jeremiah 29:11*

How can anyone not love and serve God? Now is the day of salvation, of deliverance, of being rescued from our sins. JESUS = GOD SAVES! The Church of Jesus Christ is the Bride of Christ. He is married to us! He will not divorce us! He made a covenant with us through Father Abraham. (*see Genesis - Chapter 12*) He will never leave us or forsake us. (*see Hebrews 13:5*)

"Yet He saved them for His Name's sake; to make His mighty power known."
*Psalm 106:8*

CHURH – God wants to show Himself mighty through us! CRY OUT TO HIM!

I truly believe that God was impressing on my heart, and burdening me with, the great need to pray, pray and continue to pray. He was also showing me the need for intercession. As believers, we are called to intercede on behalf of others.

"I urge, then, first of all, that requests, prayers, intercession and thanksgiving be made for everyone."
*I Timothy 2:1*

All too often, our seemingly called "prayers of intercession" have been based on our own opinions of what we thought was best for others, i.e. friends, family, church, etc. Most of us do not consult the Holy Spirit when we are praying; we do not yield our members totally over to Him so that we will pray efficiently and effectively for others.

Beloved – it is extremely hard to pray for others when our lives are in disrepair. It is also hard to pray for others when we have ulterior motives. The attitude of the heart must be in communion (agreement) with God, by His Holy Spirit. It is impossible to pray a sincere prayer for others when we have ought against one another, i.e. unforgiveness. Some Christians "use" prayer as a weapon of personality clashes! They think that they can get in the face of God and tell him all the "sins" of others, then, with great pretense, they ask Him to do something favorable for a particular person or persons. That is the spirit of the Pharisees! Jesus called them hypocrites!

Again, we are called to humility! Prayer is communication with God; He ministers to us and we minister to Him. All too often our prayers are "prayers of petition" for ourselves – gimme, gimme, gimme! There is nothing wrong with asking God for "things" – but that should not be our primary focus. He has promised to supply ALL of our needs; we must trust, believe and obey His Word.

"So do not worry, saying, 'What shall we eat?' or 'What shall we drink?' or 'What shall we wear?' But seek first his kingdom and his righteousness, and all these things will be given unto you as well."
*Matthew 6:31-33*

But what about others - our brothers and sisters who have genuine needs and concerns? What about those who do not know Jesus Christ as their personal Savior? What about a burden for the lost? What about the Church of Jesus Christ? What about the persecuted Church? (those that are REALLY going through torment because of the Gospel) What about our communities, cities, states and countries and those that govern them? What about injustices all over the world? Believe me – there are lots of "things" to pray for!

"God is bringing you into places and among people and into conditions in order that the intercession of the Spirit in you may

take a particular line......Your part in intercessory prayer is not to enter into the agony of intercession, but to utilize the common-sense circumstances God puts you in, and the common-sense people He puts you amongst by His providence, to bring them before God's throne and give the Spirit in you a chance to intercede for them. In this way God is going to sweep the whole world with His saints."
Oswald Chambers

Beloved – have you ever bowed down to pray and the Holy Spirit just overshadowed you in prayer? Have you ever wept over the sins and situations that the Holy Spirit placed in your spirit? Is there ever a time when we shouldn't pray? Jesus said that we "should pray without ceasing." *(see Luke 18:1)* Beloved – we need the Holy Spirit to help us pray!

"In the same way, the Spirit helps us in our weakness. We do not know what we ought to pray for, but the Spirit himself intercedes for us with groans that words cannot express. And he who searches our hearts knows the mind of the Spirit, because the Spirit intercedes for the saints in accordance with God's will." *Romans 8:26-27*

The Holy Spirit IS the Spirit of Intercession. He will help our inability to pray intelligently about situations or concerns. Too often, Christians forget about the Holy Spirit! We need Him every day and in every way. He is our Guide, Protector, Friend, Comforter and Keeper. We must allow Him to be our God!

"I have to keep my conscious life as a shrine of the Holy Ghost, then as I bring the different ones before God, the Holy Spirit makes intercession for them. Your intercessions can never be mine, and my intercessions can never be yours, but the Holy Ghost makes intercession in our particular lives, without which someone will be impoverished." Oswald Chambers

Beloved ask yourself: "Am I making the Holy Spirit's work difficult by being indefinite, or by trying to do His work for Him?"

**CRY OUT TODAY!**

# CHAPTER 11

### ⋮

"And we know that in all things GOD WORKS for the
good of those who love Him, who have been
called according to His purpose."
Romans 8:28

## THE WORD OF GOD IS THE WORD OF GOD!

QUESTION: Have you ever quoted scripture(s) just
because it sounded good or right at the time? Then one
day - the Word of God lifted Himself off the page(s), entered
your heart and became Spirit and Life? That's what happened
to me! God, by his Word, let me know (I'm still learning) that
IN ALL THINGS; what I encountered, what my family encountered, what the Church of Jesus Christ encountered, my "prepa-
rations" for ministry, struggles, heartaches, setbacks, teachings,
life lessons, health issues, times, seasons, joys, sorrows, fears,
storms, wish I hads and wish I had not's, IN ALL THINGS
GOD WAS WORKING! That included the good, the bad and
the ugly things in my life. These were not just "happenstances",
they were actualities, they were life lessons - and I would need
them one day. They were "steppingstones" and not obstacles;
they were there to help me and not to hinder me. They were put
in my path by the Lord! And the ones that the enemy threw in
became hurdles; they really stretched me!

"The circumstances of a saint's life are ordained of God. In the life of a saint there is no such thing as chance. God by His providence brings you into circumstances that you cannot understand at all, but the Spirit of God understands.......Never put your hand in front of the circumstances and say – I am going to be my own providence here, I must watch this, and guard that. All your circumstances are in the hand of God, therefore never think it strange concerning the circumstances you are in."
Oswald Chambers

I TRULY LOVE THE LORD. DON'T YOU? (Aww- taste and see that the Lord is good!)

THE CULMINATION OF IT ALL —

What started out as a way to vent; a way to share; a way to understand; a way to express love; a way to forgive - turned out to be the only way of FREEDOM. And freedom it is! PRAISE GOD!

Looking back (hindsight IS 20/20) - I can see, so much clearer, the Hand of God; and the Heart of God. There are so many things that I would have done differently. The very first thing would have been to recognize the Sovereignty of God! He rules; He owns; He knows; He can do what He wants, when He wants, how He wants, where He wants and I don't have to know why He wants!

The second thing would have been to ask forgiveness of God, my children and others. Why? Because I was very prideful, unloving and hurt! Hurting people - hurt people.

The third thing would have been to "cover" my children with the love of Christ. The Bible says that "Love covers a multitude of sins." Not cover up their sins! But love them, in spite of their sins; to have an open and honest heart; to listen to them and allow them to share their hearts with me.

I did, by the grace of God, do all these things, but not initially. First of all I had to remember that in praying for the Church, myself and The Body of Christ, I did cry out to the Lord and asked Him to EXPOSE all the sins in myself, my family and the Church. The Holy Spirit gave "WARNINGS" to the Church several times regarding sexual immorality. On several occasions He would stop the message and interject a warning for all those involved in sexual immorality to stop NOW! I truly wanted God to "stop" everyone that the warnings applied to. He did just that! I just didn't know that the sin would be in my camp! (And more than one time!) Afterwards, I drowned in my sorrow and pain. All my "reasons" didn't account for all my actions. I am without excuse! BUT GOD! He is a loving, forgiving, faithful, comforting, understanding, patient, and long-suffering (How much time do you have?) Father and Friend!

This does not, by any means, negate the fact that sin invaded my camp and was allowed to infiltrate the masses. I took a stand against it. I stood my ground against the enemy in the Name of Jesus. I disciplined according to the Word. I counseled those involved and received counseling for myself. I loved uncondi-tionally. I forgave, etc. These were all the right things to do. But in the dark-room of my life - God was developing the inner-most beings of my heart. THOSE IMAGES WERE NOT LIKE GOD; THEY WERE UGLY! God had to do some major sur-gery in my life; and He continues to do so. His treatment plan is precise and perpetual; He's still working on me! I PRAISE AND THANK GOD FOR HIS AWESOME WORK! He is a physician's PHYSICIAN and a surgeon's SURGEON! He took out the "diseased" parts and debrided the festering wounds of my soul! He inserted His love and promises, then He "sewed" His Word into my innermost being. I LOVE HIM SO MUCH! HIS LOVE FOR ME (AND YOU) IS OUT OF THIS WORLD! HALLELUJAH - THANK YOU JESUS; I AM NOW HEALED!

CRUX AND RE-CRUX —

The bottom line, the main purpose, the most essential matter, etc. is that there is too much immorality, especially sexually immorality, in the Church of Jesus Christ. As a people of God we must acknowledge it, confess it, repent of it, and turn away from it! If we can accept and receive the words of a man, we have never seen; believe that his being nailed to a tree (cross) could save us and reconcile us back to God; that His blood redeemed us; that He died; defeated the enemy death; was resurrected; ascended to heaven; is now seated at the right hand of Almighty God interceding for us; that He sent the "gift" of the Holy Spirit ; empowered us to live holy lives; will come again and take us to live eternally with Him in a place called heaven; has prepared the "new" Jerusalem; and that we will see Him face to face and will worship Him day and night – (YES - THIS IS ALL TRUE- AND THANK YOU LORD!) - Then why Church - can't or won't we - believe that this same God who sent Jesus to set us free can also keep us?

"To him who is able to keep you from falling and to present you before his glorious presence without fault and with great joy – to the only God our Savior, be glory, majesty, power and authority, through Jesus Christ our Lord, before all ages, now and forev- ermore! Amen."
*Jude 24-25*

If we can believe in a dying Savior, then we sure ought to believe in a Living Lord! Jesus died that we might live! Church - He is alive! We have Him living IN us. He is not hanging on a cross. Some of us put more credence in a decorative cross <u>around</u> our necks than the "presence" of the Holy Spirit living <u>in</u> us. We are walking and talking power vessels! Just think of what we, as believers of Christ, can do together!
"But we have this treasure in earthen vessels, that the excellence of the power may be of God and not of us."
*II Corinthians 4:7*

The enemy knows that this is true. But because he is a liar - he will never tell us the truth.

"He (*the devil*) was a murderer from the beginning, not holding to the truth, for there is no truth in him. When he lies, he speaks his native language, for he is a liar and the father of lies."
*John 8:44b (author's italics)*

BUT - too late devil - we already know the end of the story! Church - WE HAVE ALREADY WON!! Now we must appropriate our faith and launch out into the deep! We must go into the world; we must BE His disciples and witnesses; we must live exemplary lives; we must love unconditionally; we must have compassion for others; we must sacrifice our lives; we must be imitators of Christ. In essence, we must be just like Jesus!

"Be imitators of God, therefore, as dearly loved children and live a life of love, just as Christ loved us and gave himself up for us as a fragrant offering and sacrifice to God."
*Ephesians 5:1*

Oh sure - there are those who will lie on you, spit on you, plot against you or even seek to kill you. There will be enemies in your own camp (household, church, group, friends, etc.). But - like Jesus - we must keep walking. We too must say to our "Jerusalem" (name yours) - here I come! I know what your plans are for me, but I also know the plans that God has for me, "Plans to prosper *me* and not to harm *me,* plans to give *me* hope and a future." I WILL RISE AGAIN! So in spite of it all - we must will to do God's will. We were created to do God's will.

"For we are God's workmanship, created in Christ Jesus to do good works, which God prepared in advance for us to do."
*Ephesians 2:10*

We are the expressions of God in Christ Jesus!
I believe that the primary reason that we have allowed the spirit of immorality to run rampant in the Church of Jesus Christ is because we do not truly KNOW God, or love Him with ALL our heart, soul, mind, and strength. (Oh yes - we could be

struggling too!) This being so - it stands to reason that it would be impossible to love our neighbor(s) as (or) ourselves. To truly love God requires action- OBEDIENCE! Jesus said—

"If you love me, you will obey what I command."
*John 14:15*

Apostle John further stated—

"This is love for God: to obey His commands. And His commands are not burdensome."
*I John 5:3*

Beloved, what does it mean to have love for God? Answer: To obey His commands, which are not burdensome because we have the Holy Spirit IN us. Beloved - do you agree? (Come on- it's scriptural!) For many of us - that's another problem - INTERPRETATION! Please - believers of Christ - let's allow the Holy Spirit to interpret His Word for us!

"Above all, you must understand that no prophecy of Scripture came about by the prophet's own interpretation. For prophecy never had its origin in the will of man, but men spoke from God as they were carried along by the Holy Spirit."
*II Peter 1:20-21*

We cannot just start interpreting God's Word by our own volition or opinion. "Man's will did not originate Scripture. They were involved as the Holy Spirit bore them along as they wrote, guarding them from writing error and guiding them to write God's Word to us."
The Holy Spirit "superintended" Himself over His Word! Throughout the ages God's Word has remained infallible, inerrant and precise. It has not changed and is still appropriate – yesterday, today and forevermore! The Bible has been translated in many languages and has not lost its true meaning in the translation process. It is still the number one best seller! PRAISE GOD!

# CHAPTER 12

...

"And on this rock I will build my Church."
Matthew 16:18

**GOD ONLY HAS ONE CHURCH!**

"The body is a unit, though it is made up of many parts; and though all its parts are many, they form one body. So it is with Christ. Now you are the body of Christ, and each one of you is a part of it."
*I Corinthians 12:12, 27*

**THE MEANING OF THE CHURCH**

Literally – "the called out ones or assembly." The Body of Christ is a spiritual organism of which Christ is the Head and is composed of all regenerated people from Pentecost to the Rapture! The local assembly is a group of professing believers in Christ who have been baptized and who have organized themselves for the purpose of doing God's will.

The Church is not the kingdom. The kingdom is God's rule! The Church is the Bride of Christ. The Church has been called to advance God's Kingdom!

## THE PURPOSE OF THE CHURCH

The Church's purpose is to glorify God; to evangelize; to produce holy Christians; to care for its own and to do good in the world.

## THE FOUNDATION OF THE CHURCH

Jesus Christ is the Chief Cornerstone! He is the foundation of the Church. Without Jesus – we could do nothing! The Gospel or "Good News" is all about Jesus! The introduction and formation of the Church is the extension of the finished work of Calvary. The Cross, along with our confession and commitment closes the door of lukewarmness, callousness and compromise. We, who have accepted God's Word – ARE THE CHURCH OF JESUS CHRIST!

"That if you confess with your mouth, Jesus is Lord, and believe in your heart that God raised Him from the dead, you will be saved. For it is with your heart that you believe and are justified, and it is with your mouth that you confess and are saved."
*Romans 10:9-10*

"For all have sinned and fall short of the glory of Glory of God and are justified freely by his grace through the redemption that came by Christ Jesus."
*Romans 3:23-24*

Beloved – that's the short, yet exact version!

## FOLLOWING OUR LEADER

In John, Chapter 17 - Jesus prays for Himself, His disciples and for all believers. As believers, we must come together and say with Jesus, "Father, the time has come." It's time Church - to glorify God! It's time to BE that glorified Church. It's time to be ONE Church.
*(see John 17:20-25)*

Beloved the unity (love) that followers of Jesus display towards each other will help convince the world (unbelievers) that Jesus is who He says He is; that He really did come from God.

Listen to the words of Jesus –

"He who receives you receives me, and he who receives me receives the one who sent me."
*Matthew 10:40*

"He who listens to you listens to me; he who rejects you rejects me; but he who rejects me rejects him who sent me."
*Luke 10:16*

"For the one whom God has sent speaks the words of God, for God gives the Spirit without limit. The Father loves the Son and has placed everything in His hands. Whoever believes in the Son has eternal life, but whoever rejects the Son will not see life, for God's wrath remains on him."
*John 3:34-36*

"A new command I give you: Love one another. As I have loved you, so you must love one another. By this all men will know that you are my disciples, if you love one another."
*John 13:34-35*

## AGAPE LOVE IS UNCONDITIONAL LOVE!

LOVE is the ream and theme of the Word of God! Walking in love and in fellowship with ALL believers of Christ pleases the Father's heart. It is also the "evidence" that as believers we have "crossed over" from death (sin) to life (in Christ Jesus).

"We know that we have passed from death to life, because we love our brothers. Anyone who does not love remains in death."
*I John 3:14*

## THE MISSION OF THE CHURCH

Mission is defined as a particular task or goal to a person or group.

QUESTION: Do you believe that you have a mission – a particular task or goal that has been assigned to you? The answer is yes!

"Therefore go and make disciples of all nations, baptizing them in the name of the Father and of the Son and of the Holy Spirit, and teaching them to <u>obey</u> everything I have commanded you. And surely I am with you always, to the very end of the age."
*Matthew 28:19-20*

So believers, the mission is evident! We have our mandate. But we must have a Christ-minded mission! We must ask ourselves – Who or what is my focus? And what am I doing to fulfill the Great Commission? WHAT SHALL I CRY?

The mission (should we choose to accept it) is the cry of our hearts! To have a Christ-minded mission there cannot be any room, any hint, any idea, any notion or any acts of selfishness and immorality. The mission is not about me, nor is it about you. There cannot be any concern for one's own personal profit or pleasure – or life! There cannot be any false motives, which appeal to anyone's self-interest. There must be a kingdom agenda! We cannot have more than one mission; it will clash with Christ's mission!

On our Christ-minded mission we must be led by the Holy Spirit. "He will lead and guide us into all truth." He will show us the truth of ourselves, others and the Word of God. We must purpose in our hearts that we will OBEY!

## WALK , TALK AND WORSHIP!

When our walk does not coincide with our talk - the world laughs at us, and at Jesus. When Saul (before he was Paul) persecuted the Church (The Way) - Jesus arrested him on the

Damascus Road, blinded him with His Greatness and asked him (Saul), "Why are you persecuting Me?" (*see Acts 9:4*) Saul was actually wreaking havoc on the believers. But Jesus told him that it was He (Jesus) that was being persecuted. Why? Because Jesus and His Children (Church) are one; they are synonymous; they are inseparable! Even though we separate ourselves from Him, and are unfaithful to Him (with our ungodly lifestyles), He will remain faithful to us! Thank you Lord! What love! What grace! What mercy! What a Savior! What a friend!

"If we are faithless, He will remain faithful, for He cannot disown Himself."
*II Timothy 2:13*

This is a strong statement of the consistency of God's character! Church we too must be consistent (constant to the same principle) and always exemplify the character of Jesus. REMEMBER - WE NOW HAVE HIS RESURRECTED SPIRIT!

We must draw closer to our Lord in intimate praise and worship. It is in those quiet, intimate times with God that we truly get to know Him. While we continue to praise God (thanking Him for what He has done, is doing and yet to do) burdens and shackles fall off! While we continue to worship God (acknowledging who He is, simply because of who He is) bowing before Him, honoring, exalting Him - His presence becomes so much more real to us! He ministers to us and we minister to Him. Oh - Church there is nothing like worship! Oh - to be a true worshiper!

"Yet a time is coming and has now come when the true worshipers will worship the Father in spirit and truth, for they are the kind of worshipers the Father seeks. God is Spirit, and his worshipers must worship in spirit and in truth."
*John 4:23-24*

Beloved - are you walking in the flesh or in the Spirit? Are you worshiping God, or worrying about your circumstances, situations or problems? Can you truly do both at the same time? Can you walk in fear and in GODLY faith at the same time? True worshipers are vertical; they have an upward look. They keep their eyes on Jesus.

"Let us fix our eyes on Jesus, the author and perfecter of our faith, who for the joy set before Him endured the cross, scorning its shame, and sat down at the right hand of the throne of God." *Hebrews 12:2*

"The Lord is in his holy temple; the Lord is on his heavenly throne. He observes the sons of men; his eyes examine them." *Psalm 11:4*

Oh - the Throne Room! Oh - to press through the Outer Court, the Inner Court and come into the Holy of Holies! Oh - to be in the Presence of our Lord! Beloved - there is NO way that one can be in the Holy of Holies and not "touch" Holiness! Oh - to be cleansed! Oh - to be pure! Oh - to be loved by God!

Do you remember the Old Testament Tabernacle? Before anyone could "approach" the Throne Room there had to be a "purifying" process. Thank God we, believers, have been cleansed by the blood of Jesus! But also, we must remember that the Gentiles (non-Jews) who loved Jehovah and worshiped Him, could not come into the "inner courts". They were only allowed to worship in the "outer courts". Now ALL believers of Jesus Christ have direct access to the Father. The veil has been torn! God call us righteous, holy, redeemed and forgiven. Be a worshiper saints! Worshipers "bathe" in His love and forgiveness. Worshipers lose themselves and are one with Him; in Spirit and in Truth. True worshipers don't fake it till they make it! True worshipers cry out for the Living God; rivers of Living Water flow through them! Beloved - do you have a river or a leaky faucet? Cry out to the Lord today!

Sometimes, in worshiping God there is a stillness, a quietness – just a waiting! There is a difference between refraining from speaking and being quiet. One can refrain from speaking outwardly (with an open mouth) and yet be speaking inwardly (with a closed mouth). To be quiet is when your body, mind and spirit are under the control of the Holy Spirit, and your conscious "gates" are closed, but your spiritual "gates" are open. God begins to speak and "he that has ears to hear" – hears what the Spirit of the Lord is saying. There is no outward or inward speech; only the voice of God! I truly desire more of these times with the Lord!

## STAY CONNECTED

We must stay connected to the Vine (Jesus); we are His Branches. We must not grow weary in well doing (we will reap in due time). It does not matter how it may appear - the world's system is NOT better. They may <u>appear</u> to be having so much fun, excitement and thrilling adventures; their lives may <u>appear</u> to be very interesting and lovely; they may <u>appear</u> to be financially set (secure) - BUT the Word of God says,

"Do not fret because of evil men or be envious of those who do wrong; for like the grass they will soon wither, like green plants they will soon die away."
*Psalms 37:1-2*

Beloved - please hear me - anyone who has NOT accepted Jesus Christ as Savior is considered to be unrighteous! Okay - take a moment to let it sink in. If the believers are considered or called by God as being righteous; what does God consider or call the unbelievers? Okay - let's go back to grade school. What is an antonym? What is the opposite of righteous? (I almost gave you the definition, but I decided to let you look this one up!)

"Blessed is the man who does not walk in the counsel of the wicked or stand in the way of sinners or sit in the seat of mockers."
*Psalm 1:1*

So - who are the wicked? Who are the sinners/mockers? Answer: Those who are "spiritually" dead and guilty before God; Those who have REJECTED God's ONLY plan of salvation and are therefore "separated" from God. Jesus said—

"I am the way and the truth and the life. No one comes to the Father except through me. If you really knew me, you would know my Father as well. From now on, you do know Him and have seen Him."
*John 14:6-7*

CHURCH - PLEASE PRAY WITHOUT CEASING! So many false Apostles, false Prophets, false Evangelists, false Pastors and false Teachers are walking, talking and preaching the Gospel - among us! CRY OUT FOR DISCERNMENT!

"But there were also false prophets among the people, just as there will be false teachers among you. They will secretly introduce destructive heresies, even denying the sovereign Lord who bought them – bringing swift destruction on themselves. Many will follow their shameful ways and will bring the way of truth into disrepute. In their greed, these teachers will exploit you with stories they have made up. Their condemnation has long been hanging over them, and their destruction has not been sleeping."
*II Peter 2:1-3*

Today, there are numerous "religions" or "spiritualists" among us. They have come in with the pretense of revealing truths; showing us "another" way to God. They are bent on pointing out that Jesus is NOT the only way to God! They admit that He is a true Prophet, but deny His Deity. They are enemies of God! RUN FROM THEM – NOW! CRY OUT FOR WISDOM; GOD'S WISDOM!

"If any of you lacks wisdom, he should ask God, who gives generously to all without finding fault, and it will be given to him."
*James 1:5*

"Then you will know the Truth, and the Truth shall set you free."
*John 8:32*

CHURCH- WE MUST NOT BE BENT OUT OF SHAPE! We must not let the world squeeze us into its' mold. We must not "blend" into its pattern.

"Do not conform any longer to the pattern of this world, but be transformed by the <u>renewing of your mind</u>. Then you will be able to test and approve what God's will is - His good, pleasing and perfect will."
*Romans 12:2*

Church - we must not live according to the style or manner of this present age. We must renew, or change, our minds by the Word of God. Not by the world's philosophies, views, trends, shifts or jargon - but by a continual process of change from the inside out.

CHURCH - WE MUST GIRD UP OUR MINDS AND LISTEN WITH OUR SPIRITUAL EARS! Everyone that says God - does not know Him, or serve Jehovah God or Jesus Christ! There are many false gods among us!

Jesus answered: "Watch out that no one deceives you. For many will come in my name, claiming, 'I am the Christ,' and will deceive many."
*Matthew 24:4-5*

"HE WHO HAS EARS, LET HIM HEAR!"

There is a day coming for all of us! To some it will be a day of rejoicing! Sadly, for far too many, it will be a day of judgment! (Read and study the Book of Revelation.)

## CHURCH - JESUS IS COMING BACK! WE CANNOT ABORT OUR MISSION!

We must speak and live the Truth; God's Truth. The world, and sadly some believers, may not believe that there is a hell, but there is. (*see Luke 16:19-31*) The choices that we make in this life will be eternal; eternal punishment or eternal life. (*see Matthew 25:31-46*)

## THE FATHER'S TURN —

"Hear, O my people, and I will speak."
*Psalm 50:7a*

I believe that the greatest words that our Lord and Savior can say to us, His children, will be "Well done!" Oh - can you just imagine it? Almighty God the Father with Jesus the Savior, Redeemer, Light of the World, Alpha and Omega, The Christ, I AM THAT I AM, and the Holy Spirit - will say to us, His children - Well done!

"Oh what a day that will be - when my Jesus I shall see; when I look upon His face - the One who saved me by His grace. When He takes me by the hand and leads me through the Promised Land - what a day, glorious day that will be."

We will, in turn, bow before our Awesome God! We will receive rewards! Think about it saints - rewards from Jesus! Now you don't want to miss out on this do you? What will your reward(s) be? What we do now, in this life, will be the determining factor. Salvation is a FREE gift, but rewards are for those who are saved; they are given by God.

"If any man builds on this foundation (Jesus Christ) using gold, silver, costly stones, wood, hay or straw, his work will be shown for what it is, because the Day will bring it to light. It will be revealed with fire, and the fire will test the quality of each man's work. If what he has built survives, he will receive his reward. If

117

it is burned up, he will suffer loss; he himself will be saved, but only as one escaping through the flames."
*I Corinthians 3:12-15*

Beloved - Maybe you don't care about rewards; you can take them or leave them. BUT I DO! I want so much to please the Lord now - right where I am living today! In heaven - it will be too late to try to earn any rewards. Here on earth - where God has placed us - is our "preparation station". These rewards (or loss of them) are only for the Christians, believers, saints - NOT THE AINTS! Come on saints - God's got lots of rewards! He wants to share them with all of us. He has no respecter of person. Let's please the Lord.

"And find out what pleases the Lord."
*Ephesians 5:10*

These words are short and sweet! We must seek the Lord; search for Him with our whole hearts, then do as He says. PERIOD. It's not hard; it's doable. God will NEVER tell us to do something and not equip us to do it. Do you agree? Remember - He is Faithful!

"Good understanding wins favor, but the way of the unfaithful (transgressor) is hard."
*Proverbs 13:15*

# CHAPTER 13

.
.
.

"Give thanks in all circumstances, for this is God's
will for you in Christ Jesus."
I Thessalonians 5:18

**THANK YOU LORD—**

I n a little booklet that the Holy Spirit wrote, by the pen of a
servant who had no inkling of what to write - only a burden
for the saints - God has made His Word known to us. PRAISE
GOD! I don't know about you - but I believe that we, God's children, have an obligation to live holy lives.

"The natural life is not sinful; we must be apostatized from sin,
have nothing to do with sin in any shape or form. Sin belongs
to hell and the devil; I, as a child of God, belong to heaven and
God. It is not a question of giving up sin, but of giving up my
right to myself, my natural independence and self-assertiveness,
and this is where the battle has to be fought. It is the things that
are right and noble and good from the natural standpoint that
keeps us back from God's best.....Very few of us debate with the
sordid and evil and wrong, but we do debate with the good. It
is the good that hates the best, and the higher up you get in the
scale of the natural virtues, the more intense is the opposition to
Jesus Christ." Oswald Chambers

I thank God for allowing me these "undesirable" seasons of my life; they have made me stronger in my faith and truer to my God. These seasons have made me more loving to my family and others, especially the Body of Christ. I have a passion for God, compassion for others and a HATRED for sin! I love what God loves and I hate what God hates. PERIOD! If God says that it is wrong, evil, wicked or sinful - I agree with God. There must not be, and cannot be, any compromises or excuses on my part; even if everything points back to me! Confession of my sin and agreement with God places me in the "spirit" of expectation. I always expect God to do and be something for me. I'm sure that He desires and expects the best from me.

## MOVING ON—

What about my sons? They are living epistles of God being read by others daily. They are walking by faith and not by sight. As God has turned the pages of their lives, their father and I are watching, with such elation, each chapter being lived out in Godly (reverential) fear. God is taking them to a new level. I thank and praise God for restoration and many, many, many chances! (Speaking of chances - I don't know what number I am on. But I praise and thank God that HE doesn't keep record, and neither should we. Amen?) My sons are now ministers of the Gospel of Jesus Christ. PRAISE GOD! We are so proud of them. They are a blessing to us and the Body of Christ. They serve with us in Ministry. Many people have told us that they can see their spiritual growth, and so can I.

The grandchildren are our blessings; our gifts from God. We continue to pray for their mothers and keep close to them as well. They too are growing in God's grace. We are believing God's best for everyone. I don't know what God will do - but I trust Him! He has a perfect plan for all of our lives. I am just letting Him be God; Sovereign Lord of all! I could not go any further without interjecting God's truths:

"Sons are a heritage from the Lord, children a reward from Him."
*Psalm 127:3*

We cannot allow the "order" in which children enter the world to prejudice us or put conditions on our love; children are "gifts", "blessings" and "rewards" from God. (I had to acknowledge the "real" giver.) Some gifts come in beautiful decorated packages with bows, ribbons and gift tags. Some gifts come in plastic or paper bags without any fringes or decorations. Some gifts are anticipated - some are not. Some gifts make us happy - some cause sadness. HOWEVER- gifts (a thing given) always cause some kind of reaction. How we respond to our gifts is what matters! (Think about it.) Some gifts we eagerly accept - some we do not. BUT there is something that I learned throughout my "season"- and that is - I cannot choose my gifts. Just as the Holy Spirit gives spiritual gifts to His Children *(see I Corinthians 12)* to edify the Body of Christ and to advance His Kingdom, there are also natural gifts given to us to "grow us up" as well. God is calling for household salvation; His "House" - the Church; our physical houses and primarily our temples.

I also learned that I could not neglect, or offend the "giver" by rejecting His gifts and not offer praise and thanks for them. God has a Divine order. There is always a purpose and plan for everything that God does, and allows. We do not have to like it or understand it - but we must walk in love; AGAPE LOVE! There are many children who were not born out of, what we perceive to be, the natural order. Many of these children have grown up and are now in the Ministry serving God in all facets of Kingdom building and other areas of leadership and service. I thank God that He did not see these individuals as "mistakes". So many of us would be in trouble! Namely me! God alone is the giver of life! No one can bring forth life but God!

I will continue to cry out and spare not! My heart goes out to all those that believe someone, other than Jesus Christ, can make them whole, and holy. I pray for all of us in the Body of Christ. I pray that we will be one; that men and women in Christ will treat each other as brothers and sisters, and not defraud or manipulate each other. I come against the spirit of lust, sexual immorality, lewdness, perversion and every evil activity that seeks to tear down, belittle, demoralize and devalue the Body of Christ. I bind all of its effects and loose the power of the Holy Spirit - which enables us to be God's holy people – in the Name of Jesus! PRAISE THE LORD!

Immoralities, of any and all kinds, are not appropriate for God's children. Every form of ungodliness must lose its place, position and power in our hearts, homes, churches, communities, cities, nation and world. This can only be done by the Holy Spirit living, breathing and moving in the lives of believers. We possess the power to change! It is the power of the living, active, Almighty God. It is the same POWER that raised Jesus Christ from the dead. IT CAN MOVE THAT STONE!

"And if the Spirit of him who raised Jesus Christ from the dead is living in you, he who raised Christ from the dead will also give life to your mortal bodies through his Spirit, who lives in you."
*Romans 8:11*

Beloved we must continue to abide (remain) in Him; to bear much fruit - the fruit of the Spirit. *(see John 15)*

"But the fruit of the Spirit is love, joy, peace, patience, kindness, goodness, faithfulness, gentleness and self-control. Against such things there is no law."
*Galatians 5:22*

REMEMBER: The word fruit is singular; they are nine graces of unity! You can't have one without the others. Love – keeps them all together.

GOD'S TRUTH TO OUR HEARTS!

Beloved, I pray that God's Truths have been revealed to your heart. There are many today that believe that they know the Truth. Truth is defined as - the quality or a state of being true or truthful; what is true; what is accepted as true. If we are taught a "non-truth" and accept it as God's Truth - we are in essence "blinded" to the real Truth.

In the Bible, truth refers to what is dependable, tested and trustworthy. It is firm and never changes! God's Truth is based on God's unchanging purpose for the world and the people that He created. God cannot build on any foundation except of Himself; because He is Truth! Truth is a Person - not a series of beliefs. Jesus said - I AM the Way, the TRUTH and the Life.

Our response must be to trust in God's Word. Trust is the basis for the special relationship between God and mankind. God is always Faithful, and His promises are always true and trustworthy. One of God's greatest Truth's is that He genuinely loves His creation!

"For God so loved the world that He gave His one and only Son, that whoever believes in Him should not perish but have eternal life. For God did not send His Son into the world to condemn the world, but to save the world through Him."
John 3:16-17

Beloved, isn't *John 3:16* one of ( if not) the FIRST scriptures that we learned as children? God loves us! We are His creation; the work of His Hands! God did not send Jesus into the world to condemn us (find guilty; sentence to death, pronounce unfit for use; pronounce incurable; doom). NO! It was quite the opposite.

"Therefore there is now no condemnation for those who are in Christ Jesus, because through Jesus Christ the law of the Spirit of life set me free from the law of sin and death."
*Romans 8:1-2*

Jesus is truly God and truly man. He alone is "qualified" to save, deliver and set us free! THANK YOU JESUS!

So beloved - these writings are not meant to condemn, but to exhort the Body of Christ to:

"Wake up, oh sleeper, rise from the dead, and Christ will shine on you."
*Ephesians 5:14b*

We serve a loving, patient and understanding God. "He remembers that we are dust." and He has an advocate, or mediator and defender, for His children. We can always go to Him.

"My dear children, I write this to you so that you will not sin. But if anybody does sin, we have one who speaks to the Father in our defense – Jesus Christ, the Righteous One. He is the atoning sacrifice for our sins, and not only ours but also for the sins of the whole world."
*I John 2:1-2*

"If we confess our sins, he is faithful and just and will forgive us our sins and purify us from all unrighteousness."
*I John 1:9*

Beloved these are God's Words; they are His Truths. We must apply God's Word to our hearts and minds and allow His Holy Spirit to "uproot" all the lies of the enemy - and replace them with God's Truths. I pray that you will know the Truth and that the Truth will make you free!

"Although I hope to come to you soon, I am writing you these instructions so that, if I am delayed, you will know how people ought to conduct themselves in God's household, the pillar and foundation of the truth. Beyond all question, the mystery of godliness is great: He appeared in a body, was vindicated by the Spirit, was seen by angels, was preached among the nations, was believed on in the world, was taken up in glory."
*I Timothy 3:14-16*

# AMEN!

# PURITY

$$\vdots$$

**"Blessed are the pure in heart for they shall see God."**
**Matthew 5:8**

PURE is defined as: unmixed; unadulterated; morally or
sexually undefiled; not corrupt; conforming absolutely to a
standard of quality.

"Back in the day" – as my children would say – many of the
youths desired to be pure; namely called virgins. There was such
a sense of wholesomeness and innocence in remaining chaste.
The young ladies wore "virgin pins" which stated to everyone,
"I am a virgin and proud of it!" Those who wore the pins were
regarded as "special". Any young man knew, right away, "don't
even try it!"

Of course, there were always the so-called "fast girls." The
ones that were easy! The young men knew them and pursued
them daily. But after they "got what they wanted" – many of the
young men would slander the reputations of these young ladies
and label them as "sluts". Oh what a shame and disgrace these
precious ones suffered!

Sadly, today – to be pure is "outdated" – so "not cool."
Face it – many of us want to be cool. However there are many
Christians/believers via churches, youth groups, schools and
social groups that are crying out for purity! Believe it or not,
there ARE truly saved people of God that really want to live

holy. Sadly, the enemy has deceived thousands and the "spirit of the world" has crept into the Church.

Many precious believers are feeling "out of place" because of their choice to serve the Lord. Statistics continually report that "born again Christians", approximately 35-49% are cohabiters or are having sex with someone that they are not married to and consider this behavior to be morally acceptable! WE NEED TO CRY!

"To the pure all things are pure, but to those who are corrupted and do not believe, nothing is pure. In fact, both their minds and consciences are corrupted. They claim to know God, but by their actions they deny him. They are detestable, disobedient and unfit for doing anything good."
*Titus 1:15-16*

## SO – WHAT IS PURITY?

PURITY is defined as: pureness; cleanness; freedom from physical or moral pollution.

The wholesomeness, cleanliness and purity of sex, from the world's viewpoint and sadly most Christians, seems outdated, narrow-minded and stupid! Many people consider it strange to live a life of purity. Even most Christians have bought this lie of the enemy. They think it foolish to even consider NOT having sex with anyone of their choosing! IT'S MY BODY – I CAN DO WHAT I WANT!

The question is often asked, "How can anyone, in this culture and time, live a pure life?" The question is usually deemed rhetorical. Oftentimes we equate purity with physical sex. We only think of living holy when we are NOT committing sexual sins, i.e. adultery, fornication or homosexuality. All the other (unholy) "acts" tend to get shuffled under the rug. BUT THERE'S MORE!

Sex is God's idea and design for the human life. It is God's plan for a man and a woman, in the confines of marriage; for procreation and pleasure.

And the Lord God said, "It is not good that man should be alone; I will make him a helper comparable to him."
*Genesis 2:18*

"You shall not commit adultery."
*Exodus 20:14*

But purity must begin in the "heart" of the individual.

"The heart is deceitful above all things and beyond cure. Who can understand it? I the Lord search the heart and examine the mind."
*Jeremiah 17:9-10a*

It takes God to cleanse the heart of mankind. Purity is also a mindset.

"Finally brothers, whatever is true, whatever is noble, whatever is right, whatever is pure, whatever is lovely, whatever is admirable – if anything is excellent or praiseworthy – think about such things."
*Philippians 4:8*

The heart and mind must work together in order to "walk in" purity. What consumes your mind? Are you "setting your affections above" or beneath?

"We have to grow in purity. God makes us pure by His Sovereign Grace. But we have something to look after, this bodily life by which we come in contact with other people and with other points of view; it is these that are apt to sully."
Oswald Chambers

COVENANT

COVENANT is defined as: an agreement; a contract.

There are many churches, social groups, ministries, etc. that have adopted the Purity Covenant. The Purity Covenant is a written and verbal commitment to God that (someone) will abstain from sex and remain (or become) sexually pure in all relationships.

There are pledges that are made to demonstrate Godly love for one's self and their respectable "friend" - in ways that will allow both individuals to maintain a good and clean conscience before God and each other. There are promises that are made to protect the individual's sexual purity from the day (of signing the covenant) until the day of the honeymoon.

These commitments, pledges and promises are based on the Word of God. They are deliberate, willful and loving acts of obedience to God's commands. There are lots of believers expressing their love for God and the desire to "respect" others through this Purity Covenant.

But sexual purity means more than NOT having sexual intercourse prior to marriage. And the Purity Covenant is more than just an avoidance of the sexual act. There are many individuals that avoid sexual intercourse, yet they are still sexually intimate.

"But I want you to be wise about what is good and innocent, about what is evil."
*Romans 16:19*

Marriage is also a covenant. It is God-ordained and held in high regard by God; and it also should be held in high regard by us, especially believers. Marriage is likened to Christ and the Church. The Church is the Bride and Christ is the Groom.

God does not desire that this holy covenant be broken or abused!

"The Lord God of Israel says that He hates divorce."
*Malachi 2:16a*

## THE ISSUE OF MORALITY

MORAL is defined as: concerned with goodness or badness of human character or behavior, or with the distinction between right and wrong; conforming to accepted standards or general conduct.

Moral excellence means BEING holy! It also means avoiding the appearance of evil, in thought as well as in deed. Moral excellence is a protective measure which helps to keep one another's innocence.

As believers we tend to view evil as only a worldly characteristic. But look among the believers today and look at what Jesus had to say!

He (Jesus) went on: 'What comes out of a man is what makes him unclean. For from within, out of men's hearts, come evil thoughts, <u>sexual immorality</u>, theft, murder, adultery, greed, malice, deceit, lewdness, envy, slander, arrogance and folly. All these evils come from inside and make a man unclean.'
Mark 7:21-23

Moral excellence must be "born again" in the hearts of human beings. Without the Holy Spirit ALL of us are "unclean"! There are many "good" people that have lots of morals. However, having morals and being moral is totally different. The former is lip service; the latter is life service! Beloved – which one are you today?

## MORALITY WITHOUT SALVATION IS PRESUMPTION!

Sexual immorality comes "out of" a heart that has not been fully yielded to the Spirit of God; a heart that will not conform to God's standards. There is a saying that I frequently use when ministering to Christians in the "waiting" stage of life; "Wait – or wish you had!" In the "heat" of the relationship many individuals are "caught up in the rapture of love." I mean that they are on cloud 10 and no coming down! For these individuals, to wait would be the worst thing that could happen to them. There is no way imaginable (they think) that they could possibly be out of this person's presence for one minute, a few days, weeks or months. GOD FORBID! There is no distinct meaning or understanding to the word love. It is more of a feeling, an arousal or an attraction. BUT NO COMMITMENT!

"Do not be anxious about anything, but in everything, by prayer and petition, with thanksgiving, present your requests to God. And the peace of God, which transcends all understanding, will guard your hearts and minds in Christ Jesus."
*Philippians 4:6-7*

As believers we must wait on the Lord! We must wait for His guidance and direction; for His will and for His choice of mate. If not – precious one – you will only live a life of "if I could have, would have, should have" – a lifetime of regrets!

"For I know the plans that I have for you, declares the Lord, plans to prosper you and not to harm you, plans to give you hope and a future."
*Jeremiah 29:11*

BELOVED – GOD KNOWS!

BREAKING THE COVENANT

"Now if you obey me fully and keep my covenant, then out of all nations you will be my treasured possession."
*Exodus 19:5a*

"Keep my commands and follow them. I am the Lord."
*Leviticus 22:31*

"If you love me, you will obey what I command."
*John 14:15*

"I can't live if living is without you." Does this sound familiar to you? Sadly, this is not just a song in many believers' ears, but a lifestyle that they have accepted in their hearts. These individuals have now enjoined soul ties; they have become one!

These individuals are living as married couples; they have accepted their relationship as an actual marriage (without the dreaded paper); and they now believe that they are "entitled" to all the benefits of a legally married couple.

## SEX WITH BENEFITS – AND SOCIETY (AND THE CHURCH) HAD BETTER ACCEPT IT!

These are the individuals that do not realize, or disregard, the sanctity of marriage (a man and a woman). These individuals are self-seeking, self-absorbed and selfish. But the day will come when Reality will check in! Beloved, God has daily loaded us with benefits of his own design for us, and for marriage. I pray that these individuals' hearts will not continue to cry out – NO ROOM! But let the Savior in!

## WHAT ABOUT YOU? DO YOU SEE THE NEED TO CRY OUT TODAY?

## COHABITATION

COHABIT is defined as: live together, especially as husband and wife without being married to one another.

In a 2007 edition of the New Oxford Review, Dr. A. Patrick Schneider II of Lexington, Ky, did a statistical analysis of cohabitation in America. His analysis revealed that cohabitation is increasingly on the rise and listed five conclusions drawn from his studies:

1. Relationships are unstable in cohabitation. One-sixth of cohabiting couples stay together for only three years; one in ten survives five of more years.

2. Cohabiting women often end up with the responsibilities of marriage – particularly when it comes to caring for children – without the legal protection. Research has also found that cohabiting women contribute more than 70 percent of the relationship's income.
3. Cohabitation brings a greater risk of sexually transmitted diseases, because cohabiting men are four times more likely to be unfaithful than husbands.
4. Poverty rates are higher among cohabiters. Those who share a home but never marry have 78 percent less wealth than the continuously married.
5. Those who suffer most from cohabitation are the children. The poverty rate among children of cohabiting couples is fivefold greater than the rate among children in married-couple households. Children ages 12-17 with cohabiting partners are six times more likely to exhibit emotional and behavioral problems and 122 percent more likely to be expelled from school.

"Brian Lowery, associate editor, Preaching Today.com; source: A. Patrick Schneider, II, "Cohabitation is bad for men, worse for women, and horrible for children, "www.lifesite.net (10-4-07), reprinted from an original article in the New Oxford Review."

"There is a way that seems right to a man, but in the end it leads to death."
*Proverbs 14:12*

No matter what society, self or satan says – God says that sexually immorality is sin!
And yes beloved, God will judge this sin!

"Do you not know that the wicked will not inherit the Kingdom of God? Do not be deceived: Neither the sexually immoral nor idolaters nor adulterers nor male prostitutes nor homosexual

offenders nor thieves nor the greedy nor drunkards nor swin-
dlers will inherit the Kingdom of God."
*I Corinthians 6:9-10*

In these non-committal relationships (avoiding commitment to a definite opinion or course of action) individuals are
attempted to live committed lives! HOW SO? These commitments are bogus and they are dangerous. Is there any wonder
that there is so much confusion and frustration in the lives of
these individuals? OBSERVE!

The Apostle Paul warned young Timothy about "these times"
that we are in today. He said that some would abandon the faith
and follow deceiving spirits and things taught by demons. These
demonic teachings are from hypocritical liars – they even forbid
people to marry! (*see I Timothy 4*)

Sadly, many believers have bought this lie and are living
deceptive lives; lives that bring a reproach to the Name of Jesus,
our Lord and Savior. But beloved, God ordained marriage. And
yes, even in this age and time – marriage is still honorable.

"Marriage is honorable among all, and the bed undefiled; but
fornicators and adulterers God will judge."
*Hebrews 13:4*

BUYING THE LIE!

But there is also a casual, comfortable and cozy attitude
towards sexual purity. There are individuals who believe that
if there is no "penetration" involved then this type of "sex" is
permissible; it's okay. OH WHAT A LIE! There are many, many
ways of being sexually impure besides have sexual intercourse.
As I stated previously, purity begins in the heart and mind. Let's
look at a few ways:

1. Kissing (with noted hickies)
2. Being alone at ungodly hours of the night
3. Sitting or lying very close to one another

4. Heavy petting, fondling or hugging
5. Giving each other rub downs (so called massages)
6. Seeing each other undressed or scantily clothed
7. Visiting each other's place of residence without a chaperone
8. Demanding one's independence – I'M GROWN!
9. Having oral sex
10. Phone sex
11. Sexting (via text messaging)
12. Watching pornography
13. Writing with the use of sexually explicit language
14. Chatting online inappropriately
15. Visualizing someone in an appropriate manner
16. Taking nude photographs
17. Masturbating
18. Disobeying God's Word
19. NEED I SAY MORE!

Beloved – Can you take fire to your bosom and not get burned? NO you can't!

So – why do you play with fire? Why do we play with our emotions and hormones?

Why do we test the Lord?

Beloved – Can you really say that you are honoring God, or yourself, when you engage in these activities? Does these actions reflect Christian behaviors?

"It is God's will that you should be sanctified: that you should avoid sexual immorality; that each of you should learn to control his own body in a way that is holy and honorable, not in passionate lust like the heathen, who do not know God; and that in this matter no one should wrong his brother or take advantage of him. The Lord will punish men for all such sins, as we have already told you and warned you. For God did not call us to be impure, but to live a holy life. Therefore, he who rejects this instruction does not reject man but God, who gives you his Holy Spirit."
*I Thessalonians 4:3-8*

Again, the Apostle Paul is speaking to believers! Do you believe that God is speaking to believers today? Beloved – Are you really obeying God's commands?

"Drink water from your own well – share your love only with your wife. Why spill the water of your springs in the streets, having sex with just anyone? You should reserve it for yourselves. Never share it with strangers. Let your wife be a fountain of blessing for you. Rejoice in the wife of your youth. She is a loving deer, a graceful doe. Let her breasts satisfy you always. May you always be captivated by her love. Why be captivated, my son, by an immoral woman, or fondle the breasts of a promiscuous woman? For the Lord sees clearly what a man does, examining every path he takes."
*Proverbs 5:15-21 (LASB)*

Now if this is not clear enough – I don't know what is! God really wants His children to live holy, sanctified and sexually moral lives! We must remember that God made us and He knows every feeling, every emotion, every desire and every need. He, alone, wants to fulfill our needs. He wants all of our entire being – mind, body and soul!

**BELOVED – ARE YOU CRYING YET?**

**BOUNDARIES**

**BOUNDARY** is defined as: a line marking the limits of an area, territory, etc.

Every relationship should have boundaries (parenting, friendships, mentoring, couples, etc.). These boundaries set limitations for us; they let us know how far we can go and when we have gone too far. They also keep our relationships in a proper perspective. Boundaries help us to respect ourselves, others and our God!

God first designed boundaries in the earth to separate the waters, the sky, the land, etc. (*see Genesis 1*) Without these separations the waters would have taken over the land, etc. God, being Omniscient, knew beforehand that nature needed boundaries – and so do we. God placed boundaries in relationships, not to make us unhappy or lonely, but to help us to be holy.

When there are no boundaries in place – relationships may go awry; many misunderstandings may ensue; friendships may dissolve and dreaded assumptions may arise. Feelings of inadequacy, jealousy, envy, low self-esteem, anger, resentment, sexual immoralities, murder, hatred, selfishness and so on and so on – have been noted in non-boundary relationships. Someone feels, or believes, that they got the short end of the stick! Yes – believers have boundaries with each other! God expects believers to treat each other as brothers and sisters; and to look out for each other.

Many people are fearful of saying NO, and seek to please man/woman rather than God! Sex is a "marketing" tool today and many are paying a high price for it. Sadly, others are not even sure why they are participating in it; it's just the thing to do!

RESPECT is defined as: regard with deference, esteem, or honor; avoid interfering with, harming, degrading, insulting, injuring or interrupting; treat with consideration; refrain from offending ( a person, a person's feeling, etc.).

But in today's society (and sadly in the church) respect is becoming extinct! Too many times our feelings or emotions take over our spiritual and common sense. The Word of God must be our standard (our boundary marker). But beloved – we must read and believe the Bible to know it; and it's Author! Then do what He says!

The Word of God admonishes us to show proper respect to everyone.

"Show proper respect to everyone: Love the brotherhood of believers, fear God, and honor the King."
*I Peter 2:17*

Beloved – it is very hard to respect others when you do not respect yourself! Respect for others will not allow one to defraud others in any way, shape or form.

So – I believe that Purity Covenants are great! I suggest that we all write out a Purity Covenant. Please pray first and seek God's direction. Ask God to "create in me a clean heart, and to renew in me a right spirit." Purity is precious to God!

Beloved – if you ask in faith and truly believe – God will give you the desire (to live holy) of your heart. God's desires are always pure and holy; ask Him! Then make a commitment; sign and date the Purity Covenant; and ask the Holy Spirit to help you to keep it every day of your life. If you desire a mate – ask God! Pray for your mate – BEFORE he/she comes into your life. If one is in your life already – have them enter into the Purity Covenant with you; and purpose in your hearts to be pure before God and each other.

## WHO IS DIRECTING YOU?

As believers, we cannot allow emotions, feelings, society, peers, etc. to control us; to make us pawns. It is very important that we are guided by the Holy Spirit. Sadly, there are far too many in the Body of Christ who are performing lip service and not life service. Many believers cannot, or will not, comply to God's commands. We can talk the talk BUT we cannot walk the walk. Why? Because the Spirit of God is not in control. These believers are not filled with the Holy Spirit; they are yet carnal!

"Brothers, I could not address you as spiritual but as worldly *(carnal)* - mere infants in Christ. I gave you milk, not solid food, for you were not yet ready for it. Indeed, you are still not ready. You are still worldly *(carnal)*. For since there is jealousy and quarreling among you, are you not worldly *(carnal)?*"
*I Corinthians 1:1-3*

A carnal person is one who has received Christ, but lives a defeated life because he/she trusts in his/her own efforts, actions and abilities to live the Christian life. This person is self-directed; Christ is NOT the center of his/her life.

Sadly, on the most part, it is difficult for many believers to discern a carnal person from the natural person.

"The man without the Spirit does not accept the things that come from the Spirit of God, for they are foolishness to him, and he cannot understand them, because they are spiritually discerned."
I Corinthians 2:14

The natural person has NOT accepted or received Jesus Christ as Savior. Satan is their master; they are self-directed.

**BELOVED – CRY OUT FOR DISCERNMENT!**

But God has called all believers to become spiritual beings in Christ Jesus.

"The spiritual man makes judgments about all things, but he himself is not subject to any man's judgment: For who has known the mind of the Lord that he may instruct him? But we have the mind of Christ."
*I Corinthians 2:15-16*

A spiritual person is controlled and empowered by the Holy Spirit. This person's life is Christ-directed; the "whole" life is devoted to Christ. The life of the Holy Spirit is flowing like a river! YES – YOU CAN LIVE THIS LIFE IN CHRIST!

Beloved – without the empowerment of the Holy Spirit ALL of us will continuously live defeated, frustrated and unholy lives. It is our yieldedness to the Holy Spirit's power that enables us to live holy. He must have us and we must have Him. The Holy Spirit is a Holy Spirit! Get it?

## QUESTIONS OF THE HEART:

Beloved – Who is directing your life? Is it the Holy Spirit? Is it yourself? Is it the devil? Are you on a spiritual roller coaster; up and down; round and round; spinning in and out? Have you lost touch with the Holy Spirit? Is He lying dormant in you today? Then you must:

"Put to death, therefore, whatever belongs to your earthly nature; sexual immorality, impurity, lust, evil desires and greed, which is idolatry. Because of these, the wrath of God is coming. You used to walk in these ways, in the life you once lived." Therefore, as God's chosen people holy and dearly loved, clothe your-selves with compassion, kindness, humility, gentleness and patience."
*Colossians 3:5-7; 12*

Beloved – Do you desire to live a pure and holy life? With God all things are possible! No matter what you may be thinking or regretting – if you are truly a Child of God, by the Spirit of God- through faith in Jesus Christ – you are called to BE holy and to LIVE holy – TODAY!

"So I say, live by the Spirit, and you will not gratify the desires of the sinful nature."
*Galatians 5:16*

## CRY OUT TO THE LIVING GOD!

# PURITY COVENANT

⋮
●

Marriage is ordained of God! It is a lifelong covenant whereby two individuals enter in and promise to love, care, honor and nourish each other. A marriage relationship requires much more than physical intimacy. There must also be spiritual and emotional intimacy - as well as trust, commitment, communication; along with godly values and morals to build on. God desires that His Children live pure and holy lives; being sexually pure and morally excellent. God does not desire that anyone "try before they buy."

The Word of God has Biblical Standards to help us "walk in the Spirit and not fulfill the lust of the flesh." It is important to know that any time the Bible uses the words, "sexual immorality," it includes sex, of any kind, before marriage. God places a high value on sex and has given us this "gift" to not only procreate but also for enjoyment within the confines of marriage.

Before you sign this Purity Covenant – please consider sharing your decision with a trusted, mature friend who will help to keep you accountable to your decision. God bless you.

GOD'S WORD SAYS:
"It is the will of God that you should be sanctified: that you should avoid sexual immorality; that each of you should learn to control his own body in a way that is holy and honorable, not in passionate lust like the heathen, who do not know God; and that in this matter no one should wrong his brother or take

advantage of him. The Lord will punish men for all such sins, as we have already told you and warned you. For God did not call us to be impure, but to live a holy life. Therefore, he who rejects this instruction does not reject man but God, who gives you his Holy Spirit." *I Thessalonians 4:3-8*

"Flee from sexual immorality. All other sins a man commits are outside his body, but he who sins sexually sins against his own body. Do you not know that your body is a temple of the Holy Spirit, who is in you, whom you have received from God? You are not your own; you were bought at a price. Therefore honor God with your body." *I Corinthians 6:18-20*

"Marriage should be honored by all, and the marriage bed kept pure, for God will judge the adulterer and all the sexually immoral." *Hebrews 13:4*

Acknowledging that God has made me in His image, and that my body is His Temple, and that He has saved me from my sin, it is my desire to please Him with all my heart, soul, mind and strength. This is my promise:

I promise to obey God's commands. I promise to respect and honor God and my future mate by abstaining from all sexually immorality and by remaining pure from now until my wedding day; and even after. I promise to maintain a clear conscience before God and man; and to bring Glory to His Son, Jesus Christ. Amen.

Signed:_____ Date:_____

Witnessed:_____ Date:_____

# AFTERWORD

⋮

It is not always easy to do what God tells you to do; how He tells you to do it or when He tells you to do it. BUT IT IS ALWAYS NECESSARY! WE MUST BE OBEDIENT! That, beloved, is what I have endeavored to do – obey God.

When God, by His Spirit, puts His beloved children in the fiery furnace, His end result, or image of His children, is pure gold! God sees the gold BEFORE it is placed in the fire. We, on the other hand, cannot fathom anything but the pain. It is so hard to get past the pain, but we must. We must endure the tests and walk through the flames of life!

God desires transparency. You know – that which you can see through! He wants our lives to be open and unpretentious; nothing to hide. Why is this so important to God? It is the only way that we can be truly free! Look at the life of Jesus. He was God incarnate – YET – He had to live an open, unpretentious life! There could not be any falseness about Him. Even the details of His birth had to be open; though His mother had to bear the shame and disgrace of it all. Through it all – our Lord continued to walk, to preach, to teach and to heal EVERYONE who came to Him.

Nothing that we, as God's children, encounter on this earth is only for our own good. Everything that we encounter is to help, aid, assist, comfort, or to be shared with someone else. Nothing for the believer is hidden; our lives are open books which are read before the public every day. Some days it even seems as though millions of people are "checking out" our life's story and rewriting the book. Page by page there seems to be "entry" marks in the margins and "highlights" of those things that stand out; that cause attention. (I'm sure you know what I mean; we all have had them.) BUT GOD! OH – BUT GOD! God is always Faithful! No matter what the test – if we are ready to go through it – God will ensure that we will pass; no matter how long it takes! What a guarantee! No one else can be as assuring and reassuring and He is! PRAISE GOD!

My heart is so overwhelmed, saddened, grieved and concerned for the people of God, especially the youth. I have seen the enemy wreak havoc in the homes of the saints. I have witnessed the heartaches and brokenness of many Christian families who have been attacked by spirits of immorality. I have also felt the pangs of the arrows that seemed to have penetrated my shield of faith. BUT I THANK GOD FOR THE BREASTPLATE OF RIGHTEOUSNESS! It is God Himself who calls me (and you) righteous. (*see I Corinthians 5:21*) No saint is immune to the infectious disease of immorality, in any and all forms. But we do have a cure! PRAISE GOD FOR THE BLOOD OF JESUS!

It is my "mission" to preach the Word of God – in season and out of season. I love the Body of Christ and want to see the transforming power of God in all of our lives. I want God's best for all of us. I know that the devil is a professional, habitual and perpetual liar. BUT when we, the Body of Christ, yield and submit ourselves COMPLETELY AND WHOLEHEARTEDLY to the will of God – there is so much strength and power that the devil's strategies will not work! If we would resist him – he would flee. (*see James 4:7*)

My heartfelt prayer is that as a Body we will remain whole. When we are divided we fall. We are oftentimes divided by our own idiosyncrasies, man-made religions, philosophies, etc. We have a tendency to equate OUR way of thinking, dressing, speaking, living, etc. to be the only RIGHT way. Beloved, how we do error in being so selfish and full of pride!

The Church of Jesus Christ must rise up! We must take our rightful position; our heavenly position. WE MUST CRY OUT

FOR REVIVAL! Not a three day or one week revival; not even a prolonged revival – but a revival of our hearts. We must allow the Holy Spirit to come in and do HIS work in our hearts. We must love what God loves and hate what God hates. We must realign ourselves with the Word of God. We must STOP making excuses for our sins; but confess them and receive forgiveness and cleansing by the blood of Jesus Christ! If all the Body of Christ were to truly believe the Bible – AND LIVE BY IT – we would see a drastic change in our Churches today; and even our world. I believe that many more people would be saved as a result.

Beloved, I challenge you to take a look at the surveys of today concerning the "moral" code of ethics of believers. (The Barna Group is an outstanding resource of Christian data.) The numbers are going to alarm you. (At least I hope that you will be alarmed!) We have allowed the mindset of the world to creep into the Churches of today. Sadly, in many Churches, we cannot discern the spirit of the world; instead we have embraced it! (*PLEASE READ ROMANS 1:18-32*).) I also challenge believers to "fast" from this worldly mindset. It will be a daily fast; there is no specified duration. (Well – until death or Jesus comes!) Beloved, let us live repentant lives. When the Holy Spirit "checks" us – let's agree with Him and stay in fellowship with Him and the Body of Christ. WE ARE HIS CHURCH!

God ALLOWED me and my family to walk this path for a reason. Oh – I am sure that this was not the Divine plan that God had for us; but He is yet working out His plans for our good and for His Glory! God always has an Isaac for us; we choose our Ishmaels! BUT GOD!

# TO THE READER

### ⋮

Our salvation (deliverance from sin) is found only in the finished work of the Cross of Calvary! It is because of the birth, death, resurrection and ascension of Jesus Christ that the human race has been reconciled back to God. THANK YOU JESUS!

For many of us today, it is difficult to accept the God-stated fact, via the Bible, that Jesus is "The way and the truth and the life. No one comes to the Father except through Me." These are the words of Jesus located in the Book of John, Chapter 14, Verse 6. And beloved they are true! I would invite you to "come to Jesus" and find your salvation in Him.

Salvation is a "gift" from our Heavenly Father; His Name is Jehovah. His desire is that all men, women, boys and girls are saved from the wrath of sin. The Bible states in the Book of II Peter, Chapter 3, and Verse 9: "The Lord is not slow in keeping his promise, as some understand slowness. He is patient with you, not wanting anyone to perish, but everyone to come to repentance."

Repentance means to have a change of heart and mind about your sins, and Jesus Christ. Maybe you have gone to church, or was witnessed to by a believer of Jesus Christ, and still cannot understand how, or even why you need to be saved. Maybe you consider yourself to be a "good" person; you are highly moral and an upstanding citizen. That's good! But it cannot save you. You see beloved, "All have sinned and come short of the glory of

God." This scripture is found in the Book of Romans, Chapter 3, and Verse 23. No one can live up to what God created us to be. We cannot save ourselves because as sinners we can never meet God's requirements. Our only hope is faith in Jesus Christ. Beloved, that's the way that God ordained it! Those who believe in Jesus Christ, as the Savior of their sins, are declared righteous; freely by God's grace, or favor.

Jesus Christ died to provide redemption (to pay the price required to ransom sinners). By paying the price for the penalty of our sins, Jesus' death now frees us from our sin and transfers His righteousness (right standing with God the Father) to those who believe in Him. They are now restored to a proper relationship with God the Father; as He well intended.

Our salvation is a free gift, but Jesus paid the ultimate price; His life for our lives! Beloved your need to "be" free can only be made possible by the atoning blood of Jesus. Maybe someone has told you that you must "jump through a million hoops" to be saved. Let me assure you: Salvation is by the Grace of God alone; through faith in Jesus Christ alone. There are several Bible scriptures that will help you and several steps that mature Christians can assist you with. But please know today that God loves you! He knows where you are; in word, thought and deed. And He still loves you! Beloved – the book of Proverbs, Chapter 13, Verse 12 tells us, "there is a way that seems right to a man but in the end it leads to death." Right now you may be saying, "There are many religions in the world – why Christianity?" Because being a Christian is not just a "religious" rite – it is a personal relationship with the Creator of the Universe; it is a oneness with God the Father, the Son and the Holy Spirit. You do not have to try to "be a god" yourself; you simply acknowledge the Almighty God - that Jesus Christ is Lord; and He, by His Holy Spirit, will come to live in your heart. Beloved – you are then born- again! Cry out to God with thanksgiving for His love to us through His Son - Jesus Christ!

Beloved – if you would allow the Holy Spirit to speak to (impress upon) your heart that Jesus is Lord; and if you are godly sorrowful for your sins and would ask God to forgive you

– welcome to the family of God! Even though you are a "baby" in Christ, God has a perfect plan for your life. He will lead you in the "right path", including a Bible believing Church and fellowship with your new "brothers and sisters" in Christ. It may seem over-whelming in the beginning, but as you continue your walk of faith – the eyes of your under-standing will be enlightened. Your spiritual growth is determined by your willingness to yield (obey) the Holy Spirit. Now take your journey – go and grow – in Jesus Name! Amen.

## PRAYER OF SALVATION

Father, in the Name of Jesus, forgive me of all my sins. I take you at your word that you will forgive those who ask. I believe that Jesus died for me; that He was buried and rose from the grave on the third day; and He now sits at the right hand of the Father in heaven, interceding for me. I now ask Jesus to be my Savior and Lord. I give myself to you and thank you for being faithful; forgiving me of my sins and for saving me. I have asked and believe that you have now saved me. I thank you Lord that I am now in the family (kingdom) of God! Amen.

May God continue to bless and keep you.

In His love and Mine,

Pastor Belinda Hood

## TO MY BROTHERS AND SISTERS IN CHRIST:

As you can see, the Holy Spirit has spoken to our hearts! I hope and pray that you are "crying" out to God with me. Beloved, you know the Truth that has been declared in this book, and the need for deliverance! Let us bind our hearts and minds together and declare God's Truth to the world, and to His Church!

Maybe you have strayed from the path of Truth, and are having a hard time returning. Beloved – I have been there; more than once! Let me assure you today: YOU CAN RETURN TO YOUR FATHER! Remember the prodigal son and "come to your senses" right now, and go back home! The Father is waiting for you! (*see Luke 15:11-32*)

We need you in the Body of Christ. We need ALL the parts of the Body coming together as one unit; one family; walking in the love of Christ! (*Remember I John 1:8-10*) - "If we claim to be without sin, we deceive ourselves and the truth is not in us. If we confess our sins, he is faithful and just and will forgive us our sins and purify us from all unrighteousness. If we claim we have not sinned, we make him out to be a liar and his word has no place in our lives."

Beloved – let's not call God a liar; nor be deceived by the enemy. Today, purpose in your heart to "walk in the Light, as He is in the Light." Light exposes the darkness. Cry out to God to expose the darkness; no matter how dark it has been. And pray out of a repentant heart to the only One who can forgive and restore!

May God - who hears the cries of the righteous - strengthen, establish and keep you!

In His Love and Mine,

Pastor Belinda Hood

GOD'S CRIER!

# ABOUT THE AUTHOR

.
.
●

B ELINDA HOOD is an ordained Minister (Pastor/ Evangelist) of the Gospel of Jesus Christ. She serves as Pastor of Love In Action Ministries, Inc. located in Chicago, IL. where she has oversight of the Ministries' spiritual, administrative and social services.

She is also a Healthcare Consultant and has many years of Clinical and Administrative service – serving on a Professional Advisory Board. She holds a Bachelor's Degree in Business Administration/Management and a Master's Degree in Theology. She is a member of the American Association of Christian Counselors, and Black African American Christian Counselors and sees the need for biblical direction and guidance in the "marketplace."

She is also President of Abiding Women of Faith Ministries in Bolingbrook, IL – a Women's Prayer and Support Group - where she resides with her husband Gregory. She has 4 sons, (a "bonus" son), two precious "daughters" and (7) grandchildren.

Belinda has served in various capacities of ministry in the local church and community at large. She loves "fellowship" within the Body of Christ and believes that it is essential for the strengthening, developing, training and edifying of the believer's faith in Jesus Christ, and "witness" to the world.

She is a published author of the book, "P.O.W.E.R." It is a biblically based study to empower, encourage, enrich, enlighten and edify the Body of Christ; and to educate non-believers!

Her passion is the Word of God! Belinda has been passed the mantle of "servant" since the home going of her beloved Pastor, Teacher, Mentor and Friend –Alfred Archer; and wields the Sword of the Lord by the direction of the Holy Spirit!

Her desire is to see lives transformed by the POWER of the Holy Spirit. As an Evangelist, her heart's desire is to take the Gospel to all parts of the world! She is committed to empower, enrich, exhort and encourage families – bringing all of them into the family of God; thus building God's Kingdom! Her stance is "THE CHURCH IS NO STRONGER THAN THE STRENGTH OF HER FAMILIES." ESPECIALLY THE FAMILY OF GOD!

CPSIA information can be obtained at www.ICGtesting.com
Printed in the USA
LVOW050708140912

298721LV00003B/36/P